HOPE AND HEALING
FOR KIDS WHO CUT

LEARNING TO UNDERSTAND AND HELP THOSE WHO SELF-INJURE

ZONDERVAN.com/
AUTHORTRACKER
follow your favorite authors

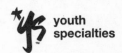 youth
specialties

Hope and Healing for Kids Who Cut: Learning to Understand and Help Those Who Self-Injure
Copyright 2008 by Marv Penner

Youth Specialties resources, 300 S. Pierce St., El Cajon, CA 92020 are published by Zondervan, 5300 Patterson Ave. SE, Grand Rapids, MI 49530.

ISBN 978-0-310-27755-2

Cover design by Toolbox Studios
Interior design by David Conn

Printed in the United States of America

08 09 10 11 12 13 • 20 19 18 17 16 15 14 13 12 11 10 9 8 7 6 5 4 3 2

TO MY PRECIOUS DAUGHTER, MELISSA.
Know I have loved you with all my heart
from long before you took your first breath.
You have brought unspeakable joy into my life.
I have savored every moment we have spent together.
There have been days I haven't been the dad you needed
but you've consistently responded with forgiveness.
Because of your kindness we are friends today.
Because of your grace I can do what I do.
How can I possibly say thank you?
Maybe by telling you once more
for all the world to see
I'll always be your
Daddy.

CONTENTS

ACKNOWLEDGMENTS

It seems inappropriate to me that a book like this would have only one person's name on the cover when so many have participated in putting it together. I'd like to acknowledge the significant role played by the people whose personal stories have given life to these pages. Dozens of men and women who have personally lived with the anguish of self-injury have opened their hearts and their journals so readers can hear firsthand what goes on beneath the surface. I want to thank particularly T, K, L, J, M, and R, who have trusted me with their stories during these months I've been working on this project. You know who you are—and you know how honored I am to be able to continue to walk with you. There is hope and healing, and each of you has given me a glimpse of what that looks like.

A special thanks to Kim Davis for helping me recognize the urgency of this topic a number of years ago. Your deep love and compassion for self-injuring kids epitomizes everything I'm trying to say in this book.

Thanks, too, to Sarah, Chantelle, and Adrian, who have helped in practical ways as this project has come together. Your friendship means the world to me, and I can't wait to see how God will use you to touch the lives of kids wherever he takes you.

Doug, I've never needed a patient editor more, and your encouragement during this process has meant more than you'll ever know. Your fingerprints are all over this book, and I want to thank you for taking my incomplete thoughts and ramblings and turning them into readable paragraphs. It really has been a joy working through this process with you.

And once again, I have the opportunity to acknowledge Lois and my kids—Tim, Norma, Jeff, Mandy, Melissa, and Jord—who have shared this journey with me from the start. You guys have always been willing to share me with the kids I work with. Not only that, but you free me up for these crazy intense seasons of writing. I am very blessed to have a family that "gets" ministry. Your partnership in all of this gives me greater joy than I could ever express.

INTRODUCTION

I'm afraid this won't be a particularly pleasant book to read—frankly, it's not a pleasant topic to write about either. But I believe it's absolutely critical that we learn all we can about this issue of self-injury that impacts the lives of millions of kids. Most adults have no idea how serious the problem has become in this generation. Parents prefer not to think about it. Schools don't have systems in place to deal with it. It's a rare counselor who's willing to tackle it. And if churches are willing to admit it exists, they see it as something "out there." It certainly wouldn't be found in our happy huddle. Christians don't deal with that kind of stuff.

But there are reasons why each of these groups needs to take a closer look. Parents are a kid's best hope for experiencing health and wholeness. As a dad of three grown children, I recognize that, in addition to the joys we've experienced together, I've also played a significant part in some of the pains and disappointments they've experienced. And I'm still learning how important my role is in helping them find healing.

Educators need to rethink the way schools respond to the brokenness of kids in their midst. The campus is the primary social and relational context for most teenagers, yet it still represents a dangerous place to many of them. I applaud the efforts of educators in taking proactive steps to eliminate bullying, biases, and social stratification, but the next step is to think about resources. Most school counselors I know are desperately overworked and undervalued. Their offices are often seen either as holding cells for unruly students or as the place where kids can get help deciding if they ought to become carpenters or architects. But the reality is that most counselors are carrying the heavy loads of many students who have chosen to share their painful stories. If we're going to get serious about dealing with issues of self-injury, we'll need to rethink the ratios of counselors to students and also provide training for teachers and coaches who are often the first to confront such difficult issues.

I dream of a new generation of professional therapists who will specialize in working with hurting kids and their families. It's messy work—counseling teenagers can be a thankless job. But it seems that the need for professional intervention increases with each new generation of kids turning 13. Of course, the development of therapists more skilled to deal with these issues will require greater focus in our training programs. Many counseling programs don't require a course in adolescent development, and even fewer address the specific issues that are typically faced by kids. It's a rare week that I don't get a phone call from somewhere in North America asking me to recommend a local therapist who'd be willing to deal with a teenager in crisis. If we could find ways to intervene more effectively during the relatively formative and teachable years of adolescence, I believe we'd have far fewer adults booking appointments later in their lives.

What about the church? We claim we know the path to hope and healing—and the fact is that we *do* have the answer. This puts a great responsibility on us. But our finding ways to share that hope and healing with hurting teenagers has to begin by recognizing that this brokenness exists in our midst. There may very well be kids in our congregations—kids of fine-looking families—who are choosing to deal with their pain in self-destructive ways.

But what about those who probably will never darken the doorways of our churches on their own? We must find new ways to open our faith communities to those who most need the good news of the gospel. We can't do this simply by inviting kids into our youth ministries. Perhaps that's the way some youth will enter our communities of faith. But until we find new ways to integrate them into the larger intergenerational body of believers, they will never experience the true benefit of belonging to a family.

This book is about helping kids in pain find true hope and healing. It's one small step toward offering these kids what their souls were created to long for. If we really want to provide this generation of young people with the kind of hope they need, we'll have to work together in ways we may never have before. The task is too large for any one group to accomplish on its own. Parents need the encouragement and equipping of churches. Churches need to cooperate with schools and professional counselors. Schools need to partner with parents and churches to provide comprehensive programs of training and intervention.

When we first met the current generation of kids we called them "the millennial generation." We were astounded by their optimism as they anticipated stepping into a new millennium that would be theirs. As someone who'd worked with kids for a long time, I shared their optimism. I was hopeful that this generation of young people might live with a little less pain than those of the late twentieth century. But just before the millennial odometer was about to roll over, we had the tragic killings at Columbine. Since then, we've seen campus massacres in Montréal, at the little Amish schoolhouse in Pennsylvania, and at Virginia Tech, to name just a few. Add to these, 9/11, Iraq, Afghanistan, the Taliban, al-Qaeda…and life starts to feel pretty messy for a kid.

But as unsettling as all those big things are, individual kids also struggle every day with the brokenness they experience in their own personal lives. Kids wrestle daily with the realities of fractured families, insecurities at school, questions about God, uncertainty about where they fit with their friends, and fears about their future.

The bottom line is this: If we genuinely care about kids, we'll want to take the time to hear their stories, we'll want to help them try to make sense of some of the confusion they feel and the pain they bear, we'll want to help them sort through their options in responding to that confusion and pain, and we'll want to walk with them toward the Light that has given us hope. It's what each of us has been called to.

A Note about Quotations and Case Studies

I've had the privilege of working with kids and their families for a long time—more than 35 years as I write this. Over the course of those years, many of these youth have allowed me access to places in their lives few people have the opportunity to see. They've told me deeply personal and private stories of events that have happened to them. They've shared poetry, letters, journal entries, and art that represented the raw reality of what their hearts were feeling at a given moment. Occasionally, when their stories, drawings, or writings were particularly poignant or powerful (as they often were), I asked their permission to keep a copy of their work and use it in the teaching and writing I do. Often, their words and images were more articulate and powerful than mine could ever be.

My deep desire is that people who work with kids would understand the issues as clearly as possible, and these first-person accounts are an important part of the process. Many of the quotations found in this book are gifts from dear friends who have entrusted me with them. I've carefully protected the identity of these young people by changing names and minor details.

In addition, as I've done workshops and seminars on these issues, I've invited people to share their stories with me if they were willing. The understanding was that I might use quotations and excerpts from these writings to illustrate some of the points being made in the book. I am grateful for the flood of people who shared their profound stories of both hurt and hope. You know who you are. May God bless you as you continue on your journey of healing, and may your words bring clarity to readers as they seek to understand the pain and struggle you've experienced.

There's another source of first-person material I used in writing this book, and it's one that's accessible to all of us. The Internet has created a forum allowing people to freely share what's going on in their lives. MySpace, Facebook, blogging communities, and other Web sites provide places for young people to post their thoughts and stories. Some of these are intentionally created as gathering places for kids who self-injure. They often contain honest and well-written reflections on self-injury.

As most of us who work with hurting kids know, the language of pain is raw and sometimes unsettling. When deep emotions are expressed honestly, the words that are used can leave some of us uncomfortable. I've tried to select quotations that will not be inappropriate for a book of this nature, but I'm sure you can imagine the intensity of some of the stuff I've chosen not to include.

I'm so grateful to all these people—many of whom I know intimately and others whom I don't know at all—who have shared their hearts. Know that I have made every effort to represent your thoughts accurately. I hope you'll find a measure of satisfaction in knowing that by passing on your stories you will help others understand a little more clearly both the pain you've experienced and your path to healing. Thank you!

WELCOME TO A WORLD OF HURT

"Stoop down and reach out to those who are oppressed. Share their burdens, and so complete Christ's law. If you think you are too good for that, you are badly deceived."

Galatians 6:2-3, *The Message*

Later this afternoon I'll be sitting down to what I know will be another deep and painful conversation with Kelly. She's 16 and describes her life as "totally screwed right now." My sense is that she's probably right. The text message I got from her late last night said it all:

i cut agin tonite sorry i tried not 2 can u plz help plz dont give up on me.

I picture my little friend alone in her room, sitting cross-legged on her bed, dressed in a T-shirt and sweats, surrounded by wads of toilet paper that have absorbed her bright red tear drops...again. I try to imagine what might have triggered last night's episode. It could have been her dad arriving home puking-drunk, leaving her the ugly job of cleaning up his mess and tucking him into bed...again. Or maybe it was her failure to fend off an unwanted sexual advance from one of the nameless stragglers who regularly flop at her house...again. Or it may have just been her inability to manage the familiar flood of pain she felt as she closed her bedroom door to the chaos of what is supposed to be her home...again.

But what triggered the cutting this time really doesn't matter now. The fact is that she has found strange comfort in the lonely ritual that has become part of her life. And I'm afraid the grip of her destructive habit has tightened by one more notch...again.

Sadly, Kelly is just one of millions of young women and men who are involved in what seems at first to be a bizarre behavior pattern with no logical explanation. These are kids who intentionally hurt themselves with sharp blades, broken glass, burning cigarettes, blunt objects, nails, needles, hairbrushes, acid, boiling water, and even their own fists as a way of expressing or managing the intense emotions that chaotically swirl around inside them. Many of them live in broken, messy situations as Kelly does, but others come from families that appear stable with no visible signs of dysfunction.

I've been meeting with Kelly pretty consistently for six months now. In spite of her sincere desire to stop her self-destructive behaviors, these relapses seem to be an inevitable part of the journey. As I think about seeing her in my office again today, my own feelings of inadequacy loom large. I've known dozens of teenagers like Kelly who hurt themselves as the default response when life starts feeling out of control. But even with that kind of familiarity with the topic, I often find myself feeling overwhelmed by the complexity of the stories I hear and the depth of the pain those stories represent. Walking with kids who self-injure can be a lonely, difficult, and thankless job.

Kelly's home situation, quite frankly, is a complete disaster. Unfortunately, I'm not in a position to change that. When she asks me if it's okay for her to wish she "had a family," I can only sadly say "yes." When she wonders aloud why God doesn't rescue her from the mess, my theologically correct answers sound hollow—even to me. But when she says, *"plz don't give up on me,"* I realize she's not asking me for advice or theological insight. She's simply asking for my presence. That's something I can offer her.

AM I TALKING TO YOU?

If you are someone who self-injures and you are reading this book, you may be tempted to compare the details of your story with the stories that appear here. Undoubtedly, you will find some common ground with the kids whose stories appear throughout these pages. But I want to encourage you to be very cautious about two tendencies I've often seen. The first is to belittle your story because it's not nearly as bad as someone else's. Your story is significant, and your pain is real. Don't put yourself down because you feel like you're overreacting to a situation that's not as bad as it could be. The other tendency is to justify your self-injury because your story is a lot worse than some of those you'll read about here. The fact that you've picked this book up tells me you long for the hope and healing the title promises. Read on, open your heart to the healing that God wants to offer you, and find courage in the fact that you are not alone.

It's a Bigger Problem Than We Realize

The issue of self-injury has become increasingly visible in the world of adolescents and young adults in recent years. Profiled on daytime talk shows, celebrated on countless Web sites where cutters can post their painful poetry and pictures, sung about in pop songs, written into the plots of movies and music videos, revealed as part of the secret world of celebrities...self-injury is going mainstream, and is likely to remain part of the cultural landscape for the foreseeable future. We can no longer pretend this is a fringe issue that occurs only in the most extreme cases. It's an unusual teenager who doesn't know a self-injurer or two. School counselors, athletic coaches, church youth workers, EMTs, probation officers...anyone who works with kids will tell us it's happening all around us, and we can't pretend it's not.

There seems to be solid evidence that the problem of self-injury is not merely becoming more visible but actually becoming more prevalent. In 1998 Steven Levenkron wrote *Cutting: Understanding and Overcoming Self-Mutilation*, one of the first books addressing the issue of self-injury. Levenkron was seeking to introduce the world to a phenomenon he believed was beginning to become part of North American youth culture. A highly credible expert in the field, Levenkron had clearly done his homework. His book remains a standard text in the understanding of self-injury. In the preamble to his book, Levenkron estimated that self-injury was an issue for about one in every 250 teenage girls—just over one-half of one percent. His book suggests that self-injury was not an issue for guys at the time. There's no reason to believe Levenkron's estimates were inaccurate. As shocking as the behavior itself was, the statistics really didn't cause many people to stop and take notice.

However, in the first few years of the twenty-first century, there was a haunting sense among those of us who worked closely with teenagers that the numbers were growing. We didn't really have statistical support for this sense that self-injury was quickly becoming a much more significant problem until Princeton and Cornell Universities published the findings of a major study done among their student bodies in 2006. Their study of more than 3,000 college students showed that approximately 17 percent (one in five girls, and one in seven guys) had self-injured at some point in their young lives. This represents an increase of epidemic proportions from the number Levenkron reported just 10 years earlier.

Furthermore, the 2006 study indicated (to no one's surprise) that most of the people who said they had hurt themselves had done so secretly. Their behavior was a carefully guarded secret that no one knew about. It seems that most self-injury is done very privately and stays conveniently concealed under long-sleeved shirts, camouflaged behind a jumble of bracelets and bangles, or hidden away on a teenager's thigh or tummy. Obviously, this means that when we hear numbers from school counselors, youth pastors, or others who work directly with students, we can safely assume the self-injuring kids they know represent only the tip of the iceberg. For every cutter who is identified, it's likely there are several others who are suffering alone without anyone to offer support, encouragement, and understanding.

A HINT FOR HELPERS

When we read statistics like this, it's easy to assume every kid we know is a potential self-injurer. I want to caution you not to be paranoid but to be intentionally observant. Paranoia strips much of the joy from this delightful ministry we have of working with teenagers. Let kids know you're comfortable talking about tough topics, communicate compassion in all you do, and help them realize you're not perfect. You'll find you have plenty of opportunities to talk to kids about the hurt in their lives, whether they are self-injuring or not.

Sometimes the Family Looks Pretty Good

Unfortunately, family circumstances and external appearances aren't always good indicators of whether someone is a self-injurer. While many self-injurers have chaotic family situations, there are other kids I know whose families and life circumstances seem stable and positive, yet they turn to self-harm as a way of dealing with something that's going on inside. The chaos of divorce, poverty, substance abuse, and mental illness that defined Kelly's environment made her self-destructive choices at least somewhat understandable. But what about those kids who come from homes that appear to be healthy and functional, yet still turn to self-harm as a way of coping?

Meet Andy, an athletic, handsome 17-year-old who is at the top of his class academically and maintains an active social life amidst all his scholastic and sports activities. When you first look at this guy, you'd never guess that over the last four years he has been regularly cutting, burning, and bruising his own body without anyone finding out. Andy came to see me only after the coach of his basketball team saw bloodstains on a T-shirt, asked some questions, and insisted that Andy needed help. As his story unfolded, I found out Andy's dad is a successful businessman with a high profile in the community. Andy's father is a "self-made man" who had nothing when he migrated to North America in his early 20s. Hard work and perseverance made him the success he is today. Andy's mom is a bubbly, outgoing socialite who volunteers at the church and in the school. They live in an upscale suburb where success is measured by the size of your backyard pool. What would cause a guy living in that kind of fairy-tale environment to hurt himself like Andy does? Perhaps this journal entry will give us a bit of a clue:

> I'll never be good enough—not sure why I even bother trying. Can't handle feeling like a loser every day. I'm not sure I deserve to be in this family of amazing people. Maybe if he'd just show up to one of my games sometime he could be happy with me. Screw it—It'll never happen. Who am I tryin to kid?

Choose Your Pain

For most kids who self-injure, it comes down to managing chronic and overwhelming *emotional pain* through the use of self-inflicted, short-term *physical pain*. The "logic" is that physical pain can be controlled while relational pain cannot. The level of cognitive distortion behind this thinking may seem obvious to others on the outside. But for the young person whose emotions have reached a breaking point, self-injury is a reasonable solution to what has, in their mind, become an intolerable situation. Listen to how 16-year-old Britney describes the thinking process:

> With each swipe of the blade or every prick of a pin I feel my pain slowly slip away, although I know it will soon return. For one moment I feel an indescribable pain pour out from deep inside. I feel all my anger and frustrations pulling away from me, escaping me. For that moment, I'm free.

AM I TALKING TO YOU?

As someone who self-injures, you may read these quotes and find they make complete sense to you. One thing I am praying you will discover as you read on is that much of the thinking that lies beneath your choice to hurt yourself is distorted and inaccurate. Take a moment right now to ask yourself how you justify your self-injury, and be open to the possibility your logic may be flawed.

To the casual observer, cutting may appear to be an act of self-destruction, but many who are caught in the cycle sincerely believe it is about self-preservation. The intensity of emotion many kids describe may simply not be visible—even to people who are most connected to them. Adrian, a 17-year-old high school junior, is obviously committed to protecting the people closest to him from the pain he is so familiar with:

> I am full of anger and hurt. I feel like nobody cares. I do it because it is easier for me to hurt myself and deal with my

pain than it is to tell someone and hurt their feelings. I would rather be the one hurting. I never want to make someone feel the way people make me feel, so I don't say anything. I keep everything to myself and then it builds up. I explode and then I start cutting. It's the only way I know to make it go away.

Anger, hurt, sadness, despair, fear, loneliness, and self-hatred are just some of the feelings that lie beneath these destructive choices. These emotions are often stuffed and denied—expressing them would represent a risk the self-injurer may not be willing or able to take. In homes where emotional honesty is not valued, these deeply negative feelings can fester below the surface and intensify gradually to the point where they must be vented somehow. When healthy patterns of thought and emotional expression haven't been learned, kids may think they have no choice but to handle their feelings in their own self-destructive ways. Listen to how 18-year-old Jasmine describes the process:

I do it to stop thinking. The blood, the cutting, gives me something else to look at and concentrate on. If I stop then the feelings I'm trying to block out come back. If I do it for long enough then when I'm done that is what I think about. Or the time has passed until I can do something else. In our household we have to be brave. Crying is not allowed. My father has a very short temper and if you make noise that will annoy him like crying he gets mad. I'm not incapable of crying I just can't. For my sake, it's best that I don't. I do it to stop thinking so that I have something else to occupy my mind in times of pain. I cry through the blood; my body cries for me.

Imagine the loneliness of someone who feels she can only process her sadness by creating tears of her own blood. Add to that the feeling of personal shame that comes with knowing that her actions are harmful, addicting, and probably self-defeating. The pain is further complicated by the realization that, if people find out about what she's doing, they are likely to pull away from her relationally because of the fear her behaviors produce. To be honest, I haven't met many people who feel as alone in this world as kids who cut.

A HINT FOR HELPERS

One question you may find yourself asking is: "Should I confront a teenager I have reason to believe may be self-injuring?" Obviously, there's no simple answer, because each situation is unique. The determining factor may be the quality of your relationship with that young person. In a relationship that's based on mutual trust and respect, you already have the kind of rapport that allows you to broach topics like this. Be gentle, asking instead of accusing, and assure your young friend that your question is based in concern not judgment.

Few people have thought through an appropriate response to the discovery that someone they know and love is caught up in this painful cycle. The first time a youth worker, teacher, or coach catches a glimpse of a freshly cut arm is often a terrifying experience that leads to lots of questions. "Should I ask about it?" "Am I the only one who knows?" "What if I say the wrong thing?" And if that feels scary, imagine the fear of parents who suddenly discover their child is involved in self-injury. Many moms and dads who find themselves in this position report feeling terrified, numb, shamefully responsible, and ultimately paralyzed. The helplessness they experience often makes them feel like victims as well. Knee-jerk overreactions can be relationally harmful and are rarely effective—the last thing these kids need is for someone to frantically tell them that they really ought to stop doing it. But ignoring the evidence is probably worse.

So what can we do? How do we point these kids to the hope and healing we long for them to experience? It should be apparent that we must not belittle the reality of these kids' circumstances or the depth of their pain. Healing will never be achieved through our reciting pat answers and spiritual-sounding clichés. There is no room for condescending judgment or morbid curiosity.

The only way to participate in the healing journey of a young person who is self-injuring is to enter their pain through deep listening, chosen empathy, and the declared willingness to live in the mess with them. That's something most of us can't do on our own.

We Have a Great Role Model

The Old Testament prophet Isaiah spoke of God's anointed deliverer who would bind up the brokenhearted, proclaim freedom for captives, and offer release from darkness for prisoners and comfort to all those who grieve and mourn (Isaiah 61:1-3). About 700 years later, Jesus read these words during a Sabbath synagogue service to announce to his generation that this ancient prophecy would be lived out in his life (Luke 4:14-21). These vivid words—*brokenhearted, captive, prisoner, grieving*—describe the world of most of the self-injurers I've known. Many are brokenhearted and grieving. They feel imprisoned in a desperate situation, sensing it can never be any different—that they will always be vulnerable to slipping into these familiar but destructive patterns of coping. It's a rare self-injurer who doesn't sincerely want to stop. But they truly believe that if they were to stop the behavior their lives would quickly spin even more out of control and they'd be left with no way of managing the personal chaos they feel. That's what I call being held captive.

What does this Old Testament prophecy about Jesus have to do with our role in the lives of these deeply hurting kids thousands of years later? If the passage refers only to Jesus' ministry, it really has nothing to say to us. But in 2 Corinthians 5:19-20 Paul reminds us that Christ has now entrusted to us the ministry that he began:

> *And he has committed to us the message of reconciliation. We are therefore Christ's ambassadors, as though God were making his appeal through us.*

This passage clearly identifies us as Christ's ambassadors, inviting us to speak on his behalf, calling people to a reconciled relationship with him. God's desire is that we would share Christ's heart for the misunderstood, the disenfranchised, the lonely, and the alienated. When we see deeply hurting people through Christ's eyes and listen to them through Christ's ears, we are in a position to respond to them with the firm gentleness and deep compassion of Christ.

An Overview of the Journey

Since effective intervention has to begin with accurate understanding, that's where we'll need to start. We'll take the time to explore what self-injury is...and what it's not. We'll discover why kids turn to self-harm and the reasons they give for being unable (or unwilling) to stop. Because of the potentially addictive nature of self-injuring behavior, it will be important for us to think through the cycle of addiction and the relationship between self-injury and other addictive behaviors. Once we have a clear understanding of what causes kids to harm themselves, we'll consider how we can help.

As you already know, this is a painful and difficult topic. But I know you wouldn't be holding this book if you didn't want to be part of the solution for someone you care about deeply. Counselor and author Robert Veninga calls each of us to consider the importance of the role we play in the lives of kids in pain. In *A Gift of Hope: How We Survive Our Tragedies*, Veninga makes a profound observation that can offer us some hope as we enter the messy world of self-injury together. He says, "Almost without exception, those who survive a tragedy give credit to one person who stood by them, supported them, and gave them a sense of hope."

I invite you to be available and willing to be that "one person" in the life of a young person who entrusts his or her story to you.

WHY WOULD YOU (SHOULD YOU) CARE ABOUT KIDS WHO CUT?

CHAPTER 2

"Most of the people around me have never and will never step past normal boundaries into the kind of place I inhabit. They go through their lives smoothly, with few bumps in their path...and even those few bumps are abstract, sterile. It makes me feel like the monster in the closet."

Anonymous Internet blogger

After a bumpy climb out of the Minneapolis airport, the plane finally reached cruising altitude. The familiar ding as the pilot turned the seatbelt sign off told me it was okay to pull out my computer and make the most of the few hours I'd have before landing in Orange County.

I cracked open my laptop and pulled up the presentation I would be giving to youth workers later that day. The opening slide announced the theme—"Understanding and Helping Kids Who Cut"— the words superimposed on an image of a deeply scarred adolescent torso. Noticing the words on my screen, my seatmate couldn't resist a conversation. "What is up with these crazy kids?" he asked. "Are they really that messed up? Don't they have parents? Why doesn't somebody just tell them to stop?" Twenty minutes later he was still shaking his head in disbelief, unable to get his mind around the realities of a behavior he simply could not understand.

The fact is that many adults don't "get" kids at all—much less the bizarre stuff that often happens in the secret lives of some youth. Crossing the gap that keeps generations separated requires intentionality and effort—and for some people the effort is just too great. But if you're reading this book, you probably have a reason you want to understand—and understand *deeply*—everything you can about this issue.

A POINT FOR PARENTS

I can't imagine the pain you must be feeling if you are reading this book as the mom or dad of a kid who self-injures. You may be tempted as you read these pages to burden yourself with paralyzing guilt. Please try not to do that! Your role in your child's journey toward healing is a higher priority right now than any role you might blame yourself for having played in the past. As parents, we all live with regrets, and we can all think of a thousand things we'd do differently if we could do them over again, but that kind of backward thinking won't be helpful at this point in the journey. Let's courageously acknowledge we are all part of the "pain story" in the lives of our children, and then let's commit ourselves to being equally important in the "healing story" now being written.

Maybe It's Your Son or Daughter. Perhaps you're a parent who has just discovered that your son or daughter is involved in some form of self-directed violence. You found a clue, asked some questions, and discovered exactly what you had hoped and prayed you wouldn't find. The intense mix of emotions swirling around in your gut is spawning a million questions that need answers right now. The helplessness you're feeling is a reasonable expression of the fear and confusion this kind of news generates. I hope that what you read on these pages will give you some answers to those questions and a starting point for dealing with what is happening in your family. You need hope just as much as your child does right now.

Maybe Caring for Kids Is What You Do. Perhaps you're someone who works with teenagers—a youth pastor, a teacher, a mentor, a youth group volunteer, or a youth counselor. Your trustworthiness and availability has given kids the confidence that's allowed them to share some of their deepest stories with you. As honored as you feel by their belief in you, there are days you wish you didn't know some of what's been shared with you. You know how important you are in the lives of these kids you spend time with. You know that a nonparental adult can be a real lifeline for a hurting teen who needs someone to lean on when life is falling apart. A lot of youth workers are finding that self-injury is becoming all too commonplace in their groups, and they need some tools to help them respond. Remember that the most important tools are understanding, compassion, and a willingness to listen—but the more you can learn about what lies beneath the drive some kids have to self-injure, the more help you'll be able to be.

Maybe Your Friend Is Cutting. Perhaps you're a teenager yourself. You live in the familiar world of math tests, track meets, cafeteria food, and book bags full of overdue homework. You spend your weekends hanging out with friends at the mall or over at each other's houses. You know pretty much everything about what's happening in most of their lives. The other day one of your friends told you she's been under a lot of stress at home and has been doing a little cutting lately. You made her show you—and what you saw doesn't look like a "little" anything! In fact it looks kind of scary. You know that this kind of behavior can become an addiction, and that she'll need your help to get it sorted out. Friends are so important at times like this, but you're not sure what to say or do next. Read on. It's important for you to learn all you can so you can walk with your friend along what may be a painful road for a while.

Maybe It's You. There's one more possibility. You're reading this because you have been harming yourself intentionally. Something sharp, hot, hard, or otherwise pain-producing has become your dysfunctional friend. Maybe you picked up this book because you're curious about what someone would say in a book about this habit that has become so much a part of your life and identity. Maybe someone who really cares about you gave you this book hoping it would help you figure out how to break the cycle. (That person probably feels helpless and unsure what they can do…other than to hand you something to read.) Or maybe you really want to stop—most self-injurers I've been able to get to know genuinely do—and you need the hope and healing that the title of the book held out to you. Whatever the case might be, thanks for having the courage to read this book and face this challenge. Admitting that you need help is not easy, but it's the first step toward the recovery you've dreamed about. No more new scars. No more long sleeves on those insufferably hot days. No more hiding the evidence. No more feeling like a failure because you gave in again. That may all sound like a dream right now, but as you learn to understand more deeply what's driving your behavior, I believe you can find the resources to change the way you deal with life these days.

AM I TALKING TO YOU?

If you are a kid who self-injures, I want you to understand how honored I am that you've gotten this far in this book. Although I didn't write this book specifically for kids who hurt themselves, I know you're smart enough and motivated enough to find truth on these pages that will help you along your path to healing. If you're doing this alone, I encourage you to find an adult you trust and invite them into your story. Tell that adult the truth about what's going on and allow that person to be a voice of hope for you. I know a lot of kids who have been able to kick this thing—but very few who have done so without some help from a parent, a mentor, or a trusted counselor. Asking for help is a sign of strength, not weakness.

YOU DO WHAT??? DEFINING SELF-INJURY

CHAPTER 3

"Scars are stories, history written on the body."

Kathryn Harrison

To be honest I feel some pressure every time I sit down to work on writing this book. I find myself wondering if I can actually deliver the hope and healing that the variety of people who might be reading these pages are looking for. This is heavy stuff we're dealing with. There aren't any easy answers, and I won't try to persuade you that there are. But if we're going to be agents of healing for kids struggling with this issue, we need to begin by clarifying what this thing we're calling self-injury actually is.

Defining Some Terms

In the few short years people have actually been talking seriously about this behavior, it's been given a lot of names. In addition to *cutting*, it's been called *self-directed violence*, *delicate cutting*, *self-abuse*, *self-harm*, and *self-injury*. It's also sometimes called *parasuicide*—an inaccurate term that gives all the wrong impressions—and, all too commonly, *self-mutilation*—a term most self-injurers find demeaning and shameful. What we call the behavior is important because it indicates nuances of understanding and, even more importantly, communicates attitudes that shape our ways of dealing with it. Most of the current literature on this topic refers to it as self-injury or as self-injurious behavior. You may find the initials SI or SIB as abbreviated ways of referring to the behavior in journal articles or on the Internet.

The title of this book refers to "kids who cut" not because cutting is the only way kids hurt themselves but because it is the most commonly observed form of self-injury. Cutting also is the most common first attempt a young person makes at changing the way they feel through the use of self-harming behaviors. As we'll discover, there are a wide variety of other self-injurious behaviors kids have used, but all are ultimately designed to accomplish the same outcomes.

In its simplest terms self-injury is an attempt to alter one's emotional state by inflicting physical harm on one's own body without the intention of committing suicide. Self-injurers seek to change how they feel by hurting themselves. And most self-injurers will tell you it works. Whether this strategy is being used to create feelings that don't exist or to numb feelings that are overwhelming, it can be a pretty effective one—for a moment. The problem, however, as every self-injurer knows, is that the relief is short-lived at best and often creates an intense need for more frequent and usually more severe episodes. This principle of the "law of diminishing returns" will be discussed later in the book and is key to understanding the addictive grip self-injury often has on those who choose it as a way of managing their lives.

The most frequent form of self-injury involves cutting the skin with a knife, blade, piece of glass, or whatever other sharp instrument might be readily available. The most common place to cut is on the arms (more often the nondominant arm—a right-handed self-injurer will cut the left arm). However, it is not uncommon to find cuts on the legs, thighs, tummy, breasts, and even genitals in some cases. Because self-injury can create intense feelings of shame, the strategy may involve finding a part of the body that can be hidden more easily.

Carving is a variation of cutting that seems to be showing up more often recently. Most typically this involves cutting or burning words or symbols into the skin—often words with deep emotional meaning that are intimately connected to the self-injurer's sense of identity. Jennifer, 16, whose parents were in the middle of a messy divorce, pulled up her sleeve as we sat at a corner table in a coffee shop recently, to reveal the words *ugly, stupid, unlovable, loser,* and *hopeless* that she'd carved into her left arm the night before. "I just put my names on me," she said matter-of-factly. Stacey, a bright, outgoing 15-year-old, had carved the word *burden* into her skin just above her knee, defining her role in the world. The word had been carved, picked at, and re-carved so often that the scar will remind her forever of how she viewed herself during her adolescent years.

Burning and branding are also used to inflict pain on the body. The superheated metal end of a disposable cigarette lighter provides one convenient and commonly used way of stamping pain on one's body, but any metal object that can easily be heated in a flame or on a hot stove will suffice. Some self-injurers even pour acid on their skin.

A HINT FOR HELPERS

As you deal with kids who self-injure, you may notice a tendency to progress to more and more extreme forms of wounding as time goes by. We'll unpack reasons for this later in the book, but be aware of the importance of intervening as early in the process as possible. The longer we ignore the problem or pretend it doesn't matter, the more difficult it becomes to deal with later.

Other common forms of self-injury include hair-pulling, bruising (by punching oneself or banging into something that will cause injury), scratching, and intentionally interfering with wounds that are healing. This last one is significant because some self-injurers report that the emotional relief they experience lasts only as long as the wound is "active." Once the damage has scabbed over or stopped bleeding, it no longer accomplishes its emotion-management agenda. Of course, the added danger here is that this can result in infections and usually results in much more significant scarring in the long run.

It should be noted that there are a number of more extreme forms of self-injury that are usually rooted in severe mental illness—including self-amputations, castrations, and the gouging out of eyes. We won't be covering those intense expressions of self-contempt in this book, because they represent a whole different level of dysfunction and require intervention that only very well-trained medical and psychiatric professionals can offer.

JUST FOR THE RECORD: WHAT SELF-INJURY IS *NOT*

CHAPTER 4

"There is no hazy line. If I'm suicidal I want to die, I have lost all hope. When I'm self-injuring, I want to relieve emotional pain and keep on living. Suicide is a permanent exit. Self-injury helps me get through the moment."

Lindsey, 15

Because self-injury is not a widely discussed topic in most circles, there are a lot of misconceptions about what might drive such behavior and thus how to respond. The anxiety of not knowing how to help leads well-meaning helpers to create explanations that link self-injuring behavior to something more familiar. The logic goes something like this: "I have no idea where to start in helping someone who is hurting himself...but if what's going on here is suicidal behavior (or demon-possession, or a simple cry for attention) then at least I know where to start."

This attempt to explain the mysterious with a simple theory that makes it more familiar and manageable may give some people the illusion that they are helping when, in fact, they may be doing more harm than good. This approach has led to a number of myths and misunderstandings about the nature of self-injury. It's important for us to examine these myths a bit more closely if we really want to be harbingers of hope and healing.

Most of the misunderstanding about self-injury begins with the inaccurate perception that the behavior is intended to be self-destructive. The truth is exactly the opposite: It's mostly about trying to feel better. While there are certainly some kids who hurt themselves as a self-directed act of punishment or retribution, the vast majority of self-injurious behavior is motivated by an intense need to solve an immediate and intense emotional dilemma. Self-injurers view their actions (inaccurately) as a solution to a problem—not as evidence of a problem. We need to remember that at its core, self-injurious behavior isn't primarily about *creating* pain; it's about *managing* pain. With that in mind, let's expose some of the myths and misunderstandings associated with this behavior.

It's Not Just a Fad

Youth culture observers have noted the way in which each new generation of teenagers cycles through various trends and fads in its quest to create a unique generational identity. The assumption is that what captures the attention of one generation becomes old and outdated and must be replaced for the next generation by something new and different. But responding to a serious and dangerous phenomenon like self-injury as if it's just the latest example of "kids being kids" is completely inappropriate.

This isn't a fashion trend or hairstyle we're talking about. It's a highly addictive, life-altering, self-destructive behavioral choice that must be taken seriously. Some in the media have referred to cutting as "the new anorexia"—and this may be accurate at some level. It seems as though new generations are able to invent unique ways of dealing with their own circumstances and the case could certainly be made for the "contagious" nature of something like self-injury. Yes, self-injury does seem to be gaining in popularity and may look to the casual observer like a new fad. But to treat it casually would be a huge mistake.

One problem with such an approach is that these pain-managing "fads" often become cumulative. It's not unusual to find a cutter who also struggles with substance abuse, sexual problems, an eating disorder, and other dysfunctional addictive behaviors that dramatically complicate the situation.

AM I TALKING TO YOU?

If you find yourself trying to deal with a bunch of "out-of-control" issues in your life all at the same time, let me encourage you to ask your counselor or a trusted adult to help you sort through them so you can deal with them one at a time. It's easy to get overwhelmed when you feel like nothing in your life is working. But there are probably some areas you could take care of (getting your schoolwork back on track; getting to sleep at a reasonable hour; cutting back a little on how much time you spend online, watching TV, or playing video games.) Don't forget that you have the power to make choices. When you start making good choices—even in the little areas—it will give you hope and encouragement for dealing with some of the bigger stuff that's going on.

Mindy is 19. She started drinking at such a young age that she can't remember a time before she drank. By the time she was 12, she realized alcohol had become a serious problem. By then she'd already begun dabbling casually in the drug scene. Before the end of her freshman year of high school, she was using whatever she could get her hands on. It was about this time she began to experiment with cutting on her upper arms and thighs. She told me she probably wouldn't have thought of it, but her older sister—who'd been cutting secretly for several years—showed her how to do it. All this was going on while her family was falling apart. By the time she was 16, she'd had at least one pregnancy that ended in a miscarriage and was binging and purging in an endless bulimic cycle. Where do you start with a kid like Mindy? For her, cutting is just one facet of a desperate and vicious cycle of pain management. We dare not dismiss this growing problem as a fad that will surely disappear when kids get tired of it.

It's Not an Extreme Version of Tattoos and Lip Rings.

Body modification is big business these days. Primetime TV shows give us an inside look at the patrons and tattoo artists who make up that interesting world. Body mod shops have found their way into the local mall. If you work much with kids, you probably don't give a second thought to piercings, tattoos, and other expressions of uniqueness that are common for this generation. I suppose some people might argue that tattoos and piercings are an assault on the skin and that self-injurious behavior is, therefore, somehow closely related. And it may very well be that a self-injurer you know also has tattoos or piercings. But a closer look will show a substantial difference between the motivations for the two behaviors.

Those who engage in body modification like tattoos and piercings do so to create a look they find more interesting or attractive, or perhaps to express their uniqueness in a world where everything seems to look the same. Self-injurers know their wounds are not attractive. In fact, most do everything they can to hide their scars. What a difference from those who have invested big bucks in tattoos and piercings and love to show them off for the world to see. Self-injury is not merely body modification taken to an extreme.

By the way, I'm not suggesting that all body modification is appropriate or that it should never be a cause for concern. Some of the more extreme forms of body modification emerging probably do require that we take a second look and try to understand the motivation behind them.

It's Probably Not a Suicide Attempt…Yet

It's not surprising that one of the most common misunderstandings about self-injuring behavior is that it represents a suicidal gesture. After all, it often involves behaviors that look very "suicide-like"—knives, wrists, blood. But nothing could be further from the truth for most self-injurers. Most kids who cut describe their behavior as a calculated and deliberate survival strategy. It's their desperate attempt to make it through another day—not to end it all.

When self-injurious behavior began to be more common a few years ago, it was often addressed as if it were some sort of death wish. Self-injurers were routinely placed on suicide watch in hospital psychiatric wards and treated as though their desire was to end their lives. For most of them, this simply increased their sense of shame and reminded them of how misunderstood they were. How much more helpful to acknowledge and affirm their intense desire to live and to help them find more appropriate ways to accomplish that outcome.

There is one problem, however, that must be acknowledged when we suggest that self-injury typically has no suicidal intent. Self-injuring is a response to deep pain, brokenness, betrayal, abandonment, despair, and depression—yet it can't possibly address those underlying problems adequately. Ultimately, this can lead self-injurers to deeper and deeper feelings of hopelessness, fear, and gloom. At some point these increasing feelings of pain and the recognition that the self-injurious behavior is failing to relieve them, may lead to the kind of desperation that could express itself in suicide.

Don't hesitate to have a frank conversation with a self-injurer you know about whether he or she is slipping toward that level of hopelessness. As is true with any suicide intervention, asking the question, "Are you now or have you ever been at a point where you are thinking about taking your own life?" is the appropriate thing to do. Asking this question will not plant suicidal thoughts in a young person's mind; in fact, in most cases teenagers thinking seriously about suicide will be relieved to know someone is willing to discuss it with them. For a more thorough discussion of how to respond to a suicidal teenager, I'd suggest *The Youth Worker's Guide to Helping Teens in Crisis* by Jim Hancock and Rich Van Pelt (Zondervan, 2005).

A HINT FOR HELPERS

You might be interested to know that some of the people who study and interpret statistics about "suicide attempts" are wondering if many incidents that were originally counted as attempted suicides were actually kids who were self-injuring. Obviously, the intervention necessary for a suicide attempt is substantially different from what is needed in the case of self-injury.

It's Not Demon Possession

Another commonly held myth about self-injury sees the behavior as clear evidence of demon possession. After all, how could something so bizarre and self-destructive be anything other than the explicit and intentional work of Satan? Besides, wasn't there a demon-possessed guy in the Bible who used to cut himself with stones until Jesus healed him and sent those demons into the lake courtesy of a nearby herd of pigs? (Mark 5:1-20). And what about those worshippers of Baal who took on Elijah in a fire-starting contest and slashed themselves with swords and spears in their frenzied failure to ignite? (1 Kings 18:20-40). That certainly had the look of demonic activity. Isn't the same thing going on with these kids?

Well, let's be careful we don't violate the basic laws of logic here. The fact that someone who was demon-possessed chose to harm themselves with sharp stones or knives by no means implies that all people who harm themselves are demon-possessed. Given what we know about the Enemy of our souls, it's not a stretch to think that he might be involved in facilitating something as destructive as self-injury. But let's not assume these kids are possessed by Satan.

The issue of demonic involvement in human life has been hotly debated for thousands of years. It's not my purpose to take on this complex theological issue here, but let me offer a few observations. Most Christians acknowledge the existence of a spiritual world, the dark side of which is described in Ephesians 6:12, where Paul refers to "the spiritual forces of evil in the heavenly realms." Unfortunately, most of us are not consciously aware of the day-to-day reality of this battle. As long as things are going relatively well, we make the assumption that we really don't need to worry about the Enemy of our souls. That may be why when we do think about Satan's involvement in people's lives, the terminology we often use is that of demonic "possession." In most cases the assumed solution for this level of spiritual warfare involves a confrontational exorcism, or "deliverance." The truth of the matter is that the Bible describes Satan and his helpers in much more generic terms—prowling, accusing, testing, opposing, lying, and generally making the life of the believer miserable in every way they can. There is no question in my mind that the phenomenon of self-injury is tangled up in the day-to-day reality of spiritual warfare, and that appropriate spiritual responses must ultimately be part of a complete healing. But I believe it would be inappropriate to assume that every adolescent who self-injures is in need of an exorcism.

It's Not Just an Attempt to Get Attention

Whether you're a parent, a teacher, or a youth worker, one of the great challenges of working with kids is responding appropriately to attention-seeking behavior. The fact is that some youngsters use relationally destructive behaviors in an unhealthy attempt to create relationship—or "involvement" as I prefer to understand it. Perhaps some teenagers are so intensely desperate for involvement that they resort to self-injuring behavior. But what concerns me about this "diagnosis" is that the response to negative behavior understood as attention-seeking is typically to withhold attention. Obviously, we don't want to reinforce unhealthy patterns of attention-seeking. But when we find ourselves in relationship with a young person whose relational style clearly begs for involvement, we need to take the time to hear and understand the backstory.

Many of the cutters I know come from situations marked by betrayal, abandonment, and brokenness. Their need for relational affirmation is very real and, in many cases, quite urgent. They may have learned in their dysfunctional environments that the only way to get that sort of involvement is to be in crisis or to create an emergency of some sort. To ignore such a desperate cry for help simply because we believe it's an attempt to get attention may leave a young person feeling as if they need to do something even more extreme to get someone to notice.

So what's the appropriate response when we discern that a youth's self-injurious behavior is *just* an effort to seek attention? The first thing we must do is to remove the word *just* from the sentence. That word belittles the reality of the pain many of these kids are in. Listen to what Jesse says in his journal:

I was always alone. My dad didn't come home until after I was in bed and he was usually still asleep when I left in the morning. My mom worked shifts so she was either at work or sleeping whenever I came home from school. When they found out that I was cutting, my mom freaked out and took two weeks off work. But then after the two weeks were done she had to go back and I lost her again. I think I kept doing it just to see if either of them would notice. They didn't.

A POINT FOR PARENTS

Here's one of those places where you might find it easy to head out on a guilt trip. But instead of focusing on what you did or didn't do in the past, I want to challenge you to try to find practical ways you can offer your son or daughter a little more attention right now. Are there ways you could spend more time together? Is there an activity that both of you enjoy that you could get involved with? Could you make some adjustments to your work schedule to be a little more available to your child than you've been recently? Remember that something is always better than nothing, and now is always better than later. There is no one more important in the life of your teenager than you!

When kids use self-injury as a means of getting attention, it's important for them to be reassured that what they long for is right and good and legitimate. The involvement Jesse and kids like him long for from their families is completely appropriate; it's the method Jesse has chosen to make the request that is not. It's not wrong to want the attention and care of a parent or friend. But in the absence of positive relational involvement, lonely kids will often assume it is actually their deep need for love, attention, affirmation, and time that is the problem. These kids begin to disdain the longing that drives them. Sadly, the only way to express that disdain is to become emotionally numb and dead inside...and when you're dead nothing really hurts, does it?

In *Hurt: Understanding the World of Today's Teenagers* (Baker, 2004), author Chap Clark tells us we are working with a generation of youth who have been systemically abandoned by family, their communities, and the church. If this is true—and I have every reason to believe Chap is right—we'd better get used to working with kids who are going to use all sorts of extreme measures to try to get involvement from the adults who mean the most to them.

It *IS* a Big Deal

Perhaps the most dangerous potential response to a self-injuring teen is for us to brush the behavior off as a silly, childish whim and assume it will simply go away or they'll grow out of it (after just a few minor incidents, we hope). It is certainly possible that some teenagers will make a first attempt at self-harm, find that it's unsatisfying or hurts more than expected, and never try it again. Perhaps there are youth who will experiment with cutting, recognize the addictive potential of the behavior, and move on to some other coping mechanism. But I would suggest that hoping the behavior will simply disappear on its own is probably not a helpful approach. Self-injury does not happen in a vacuum—it is driven by some form of unhealthy thinking. Maybe it's being used as an inappropriate way of dealing with pain; maybe the cutter is so socially insecure that peer pressure pushes them into it; or maybe he or she is unable to recognize the potential dangers of such self-destructive behavior. Whatever the case, it would be entirely inappropriate for a caring adult to ignore it.

We've spent some time in this chapter challenging some of the misunderstandings that surround the phenomenon of self-injury. We cannot belittle it as a passing fad, nor can we chalk it up to piercings that have gone wild. In most cases it's not a botched suicide attempt and, while Satan may be involved, it's likely not demon-possession that drives most kids. Clearly, we shouldn't blow it off as nothing more than an attention-getting device or a silly one-time experiment. Instead, we must learn to spot the signs of self-injury, understand the real motivations for the behavior, and then discover how to respond appropriately. That's what the rest of this book is all about.

AM I TALKING TO YOU?

I've often asked teenagers who are deeply involved with self-injuring behavior what they would say to any kids who have just started to hurt themselves as a way of dealing with their pain. I wish I could communicate to you how passionately every one of them has told me they'd tell any kid who's just starting to cut to stop while it's still possible. If you've just begun dabbling in self-injury, I want to challenge you to recognize the seriousness of this behavior that often becomes a powerful addiction. Get help while you can. You'll be glad you did.

TOO HOT FOR LONG SLEEVES? RECOGNIZING THE SIGNS

"I guess I don't think about the scars when I'm doing it. It just happens in the moment—I'm not thinking about what it will look like a month later...and now I have to spend the rest of my life covering up the ugliness of it."

Abbey, 17

Shaina's mom was unraveling in front of me. I was a rookie youth pastor, and I'd just wrapped up a parent meeting by telling folks I was available to discuss any issues they felt I might be able to help with. She was the first one to the front to talk. With tears streaking her cheeks she asked, "How could I have missed it? Shaina told me it's been going on for over a year. Why wasn't I paying closer attention?" A single parent with two teenagers, Shaina's mom was juggling a lot, including her own confusion about the messy breakup of her marriage about six months earlier. Just the day before she'd noticed some blood-soaked wads of tissue that had fallen behind her 14-year-old daughter's bed. At first Shaina had tried to explain it away with a vague story about hurting her leg at a volleyball practice, but her mom wouldn't buy it. It wasn't long before the dreaded truth came out. Now intense feelings of fear, anxiety, and guilt were combining to create a hopelessness that most parents feel when they find out their child has been self-injuring.

I felt sorry for Shaina's mom because of the shame she felt for having missed the signs of her child's struggle. But as many of us know, symptoms are always much clearer in the rearview mirror. Whether we're talking about a medical condition, an addiction, or even a suicide, in retrospect there is often a sense that we should have seen it for what it was—we just didn't.

Let's Just Pretend Everything's Okay

Perhaps part of the problem is that we don't actually want to know this kind of disturbing news about someone we love. I know that my natural tendency as a parent is to deny the reality of what's going on in the lives of my own kids. There are a variety of reasons why we'd rather pretend everything is all right.

For parents, when it comes to the possibility that our own child may be self-injuring, one big reason for denial is we really don't know what to do if we find that something serious is wrong. Add the feelings of failure that come with believing we are somehow responsible for the problem, along with the embarrassment of others finding out, and there are plenty of reasons for denying the truth. But we must find the courage to face reality—especially when the emotional, spiritual, and physical health of our kids is at stake.

Clues That Something May Be Wrong

Whether you're a parent, an adult who works with kids, or a friend who wants to be equipped to provide help and support to someone who is self-injuring, you need to be aware of the signs that someone may be self-injuring. The indicators on the next few pages are by no means comprehensive or complete, and some of the signs mentioned here could be related to something other than self-injury. But if you see more than a few of these signals, you should probably be concerned.

- ### *Scars, unexplained cuts, bruises, or burns*
  This is the obvious place to start. Even though it would seem unlikely that something as apparent as unexplained skin damage or scabs and scars would be overlooked, I am amazed at how often these signs go unnoticed or ignored. Kids will come up with excuses to explain their cuts and bruises—and perhaps on first occasion they should be given the benefit of the doubt. But if these signs are seen over and over, they simply cannot be denied. The most common places for seeing cuts or burns are the arms and thighs. Other kids may choose areas of the body that are less likely to be accidentally exposed, such as tummies and breasts.

- ### *Wearing long-sleeved shirts or long pants when the weather or occasion calls for something lighter*
  "Why don't you put on something a little cooler? You look like you're roasting in that." Summertime means shorts and T-shirts for most teens, but for self-injurers those may simply not be options. Their highest priority is protecting their secret, not caring for their own personal comfort. Kids who cut themselves face the ongoing dilemma of having to hide their scars from people around them. The shame they feel about their self-injury often grows from the stares and snickers of the people who have seen the evidence. Unfortunately, even when the wounds have healed, they leave telltale scars that have to be guarded for the rest of one's life. One reason kids continue cutting is because they sense that the damage has already been done—their arms or legs are already scarred permanently and that harm

can't be undone. The hopelessness this induces may well be another reason why kids who cut hide behind clothing that not only covers their wounds but also protects them from being seen or known.

AM I TALKING TO YOU?

Looking at the scars on your body may leave you feeling hopeless. You may think there's no point in stopping your self-injury now, because you're already scarred. Can I challenge your thinking? One day you're going to stop hurting yourself. The less damage you've done, the easier it will be to get on with your life when that time comes. Scars do fade over time, and so will some of the memories of this painful time in your life. Don't believe the lie that says because there are already so many scars, a few more won't matter. Every time you choose not to hurt yourself, you've scored a personal victory. Enjoy those victories and realize you're making it easier for yourself in the future.

- *Bangles, bracelets, wristbands*

  Like the long-sleeved shirts, these accessories may be a fashion statement—and if they are, that's great. But cutters will often use multiple bracelets or wristbands as a way of hiding minor cuts and scars on their arms. Simply being observant enough to notice what's being hidden could lead to a really important conversation.

- *Broken disposable razors*

  Perhaps the most easily accessible sharp objects in most homes are the tiny blades found in disposable razors. Self-injuring teens have often told me this is their instrument of choice. The head of the razor is simply broken to provide a blade that can be used for a cutting episode and then easily disposed of. But kids may not remember to get rid of the broken razor their blade was taken from. Parents who find disposables with their blades removed should probably be alert for other signs that would confirm their concerns.

- *Collections of cutting paraphernalia*

  Most young people don't have collections of knives, box cutters, X-Acto blades, and other cutting objects, but some kids who self-injure keep such collections and may find they bring comfort even when they're not being used. Carrying a prized knife at all times gives the self-injurer a sense of control—if something should go emotionally or relationally wrong, he or she has the option of taking care of it immediately. Some kids have a favorite blade, others find comfort in having a collection of options.

A HINT FOR HELPERS

One practical way you can help a cutter is by asking if that young person has a favorite knife (or collection of knives), and seeing if he or she would be willing to hand it over to you. Handing over a knife represents a tangible step in the journey toward quitting and an important way self-injurers can feel a sense of ownership in their own recoveries. Even though you and the cutter both know there are all sorts of other options, this can be a really significant step toward healing. You'd be amazed at the bizarre collection of knives and razors I have in my office drawer, each one representing a small step of victory for the kid who gave it to me.

There can be some very distorted thinking behind these collections. Because cutting never provides long-term relief for the pain it is meant to address, for some cutters, each instrument of injury represents an attempt to alleviate the hurt inside—and they may think a change in blades might be the answer. I once got a call from a kid who was trying to decide which of more than dozen options she ought to use for the harm she was about to inflict on her body. She described in detail several knives, two pairs of scissors, five or six different razors, some shards of broken glass, and a few really sharp stones. The statement she made to me after outlining her options told the whole story:

> I'm just trying to figure out which one of these will hurt the longest and take the most time to heal. My favorite old knife just isn't doing it for me anymore.

- ### Knives, scissors, or tools found unexpectedly in a teenager's room

  Sometimes this can be explained: "I was cutting up an apple while I was talking on the phone..." "I needed to cut pictures out of a magazine for a school project..." "I was scrapbooking..." But when there is a repeated pattern of finding sharp objects or cutting instruments in a child's room, something more may well be going on.

- ### Bloodied wads of tissue or toilet paper, or blood on towels, facecloths, etc.

  Again there may be an explanation (a nosebleed, a shaving accident, etc.) but if the pattern persists and the excuses start to seem unbelievable, it might be worth further exploration. Pay particular attention to bloodstains that appear to be in the shape of a line—in the early stages of cutting, wounds may not be deep enough to generate much beyond oozing.

- ### First-aid supplies or antiseptic ointments near the bed or being used in the bathroom

  Most self-injurers are quite careful about keeping their cuts from getting infected. It isn't unusual for them to be as meticulous about caring for their injuries as they were about inflicting them in the first place. This means using creams, sprays, Band-Aids, gauze, and other first-aid materials. If you see this sort of stuff lying around a young person's room or being used more often than normal, it would be worthwhile to check for other signs or even to ask some questions. Be prepared for evasive answers if self-injury is occurring. (By the way, if you are providing care and support for someone who self-injures, make sure that person has access to adequate first-aid supplies so they can take appropriate care of themselves.)

AM I TALKING TO YOU?

If you are cutting, or hurting yourself in some other way, let me remind you how important it is to take care of yourself afterward. Make sure you keep your wounds clean so they can heal. Remember that one day your heart will heal too. If you ever find yourself having been more aggressive than usual, let someone you trust look at what you've done and help you decide if you need medical attention. You can't do this alone.

- *Traces of blood on clothing, especially the inside of shirt sleeves or pant legs, bras, tummy area of shirts, etc.*
  In spite of the care most kids take, cuts will continue to bleed for a while and often leave telltale signs that can be noticed in the laundry basket—or, more likely, in that giant pile of dirty clothes that seems to exist in the corner of every teenager's room. I'm not suggesting parents should constantly be checking their kids' clothes for signs of anything suspicious, but in the routine of living under the same roof, we should be aware enough to notice these sorts of things and wise enough to know how to respond if we find something that causes concern.

- *Rubbing arms—especially wrists—through sleeves*
  Cuts are usually itchy when they are healing. Very often self-injurers will absentmindedly rub their arms or legs as a form of self-care. A combination of long-sleeved shirts

and constant rubbing of the arms may be an indication there are some cuts healing underneath those sleeves. Obviously, an itchy arm or leg is no reason to panic, but in combination with some of the other signs mentioned, it may indicate a problem worth noting.

• *The emotional roller coaster*

Because of the intense emotions that often drive self-injurious behavior and the immense and immediate relief that comes with a cutting episode, it is not unusual to notice extreme emotional cycles among some self-injurers. Of course, emotional ups and downs are a normal part of the adolescent experience, so this symptom is not particularly helpful on its own. But when found in combination with some of the other symptoms we've mentioned, it may be an indicator. The sad reality is that many parents are oblivious to what's going on emotionally in the lives of their kids. To be really tuned in to the ups and downs requires that we be intentionally present and relationally connected at a significant level. There are no simple ways to accomplish this other than to offer availability, authenticity, and acceptance—the everyday stuff of good parenting.

WHAT ARE THEY THINKING?

CHAPTER 6

"I urge you, brothers and sisters, in view of God's mercy, to offer your bodies as a living sacrifice, holy and pleasing to God—this is true worship. Do not conform to the pattern of this world, but be transformed by the renewing of your mind."

Romans 12:1-2

If lives are transformed by the renewing of the mind, then it's important for us to understand how the teenage mind actually works. Once we have a sense of how most kids think, we'll have a foundation in place for understanding some of the distorted thinking that leads to self-injury.

We'll discover in this chapter that adolescents are experiencing massive transitions in the way their brains process and interpret information, and that some of those transitions have a direct relationship to our understanding of self-injury. At times it seems as if teenagers sporadically switch back and forth between immature childlike thinking and the more sophisticated cognitive processes of an adult—and to a large extent this is true. What are the implications of all this cognitive chaos, especially in light of some of the other important transitions that are going on for a teenager?

A great deal is being discovered about the way the adolescent brain functions both neurologically and practically. The topic is far too complex to tackle comprehensively in a book like this, but there are some fundamental things we should be aware of if we want to understand the distorted thinking that often drives behaviors such as self-injury.

A quick Internet search of "adolescent brain development" will generate links to all sorts of good resources for understanding some of the research being done in this important area. The work being done by Dr. Jay Giedd at the National Institute of Mental Health in Bethesda, Maryland, is particularly valuable in helping us understand at least some of the factors related to self-injury. For example, Giedd and his team discovered that one of the last parts of the adolescent brain to develop is the area related to discernment and understanding consequences. Basically, Giedd's research indicates that adolescents are, for all intents and purposes, neurologically incapable of consistently processing the "What will happen next?" question. The operative word here is *consistently*. At times adolescents seem to know exactly what will happen next; at other times we may shake our heads in amazement at their apparent lack of foresight.

When kids are living with emotional stresses and unresolved pain, their capacity to think about the implications of their actions may very well be reduced even further. For those of us who find ourselves asking, "What were you thinking?" it's important to understand a little bit more about how kids process events and circumstances in their lives. The truth is, they may not have been thinking consciously at all.

Giedd suggests that many people do not fully realize this capacity to process consequences until their early twenties.

Because the average age of onset for self-injury is around 14, these negative behavioral patterns can be firmly in place long before a kid has the ability to think through the implications of the solution they've chosen to deal with their pain. It's just another reminder of how important it is for young people to have objective voices in their lives to assist them in making sense of their choices.

A POINT FOR PARENTS

One way we can help our kids develop more mature thinking is to make sure they understand the connection between their choices and the consequences of those choices. It has been said that we are the generation of parents who "prepares the road for our children instead of preparing our children for the road." We don't do our kids any favors when we absorb or deflect the consequences of even the little choices they make. We can help them grow to be responsible adults by allowing them to live with the outcomes of their own choices.

Not a Child Anymore

There is another developmental reality in the thinking process of adolescents that's a little more complicated but nevertheless crucial for us to understand. It has to do with the somewhat unpredictable but inevitable transition from childlike thinking to adult thinking that takes place during adolescence. It's no secret there are fundamental differences between the way a child thinks and the way an adult thinks. Developmental psychologists like Jean Piaget have researched and documented these differences. In simple terms children tend to think more concretely, while adults have the capacity to think more abstractly or conceptually. Children tend to experience life as black and white, straight lines, and consistent. Nuances and subtleties are generally beyond their capacity to interpret. Most adults, on the other hand, recognize that life is shades of gray, tangled, and unpredictable. Our lived experience is marked by nuance and leaves a lot of room for subjective interpretation. Adults are generally able to wrestle with opposing viewpoints, to think about possibilities, to generate ideas, and to come to conclusions without tangible evidence.

It is during adolescence that the transition from childlike thinking to the more complex form of adult thinking is being made. One way to visualize this transition is by imagining adolescence as a bridge. One end of this bridge called adolescence is planted in the safe world of childhood; the other extends onto the much more complicated shore of adulthood. Often a teenager will run back and forth between the sophisticated cognitive processes of the adult and the much simpler approach of a child. Some parents and others who work with teens may find this highly frustrating, but for the young person it represents a way to stay safe in situations that are confusing, painful, or volatile. When thinking like an adult is too risky or has more costly implications, kids will often revert to safer childlike thinking where emotions are less intense and the responsibility to act on what is known is not as great.

The transition from childlike thinking to adult thinking expresses itself in at least one other important way. This has to do with the way people interpret life's events. Children tend to experience life as a series of isolated, consecutive occurrences. These occurrences may be intense, traumatic, and life-shaping. If the events in a child's life are negative, they may do great damage to a child's soul. But children tend to be amazingly resilient—when the sun comes up the next morning, a new day has begun and life goes on. In early adolescence this pattern changes. The developing brain begins to have the capacity to create what might be called an "integrated personal history." This means adolescents gain the ability to link a series of events together, to find themes that make sense of what's happening.

For example, events that generated emotions of loneliness or feelings of abandonment are linked together and become a thread that ties an individual's personal story together. The same might be true of events that generate feelings of inadequacy, fear, shame, or sadness. These themes become the foundation for identity formation.

Who Am I?

Here's where we add one more variable to this already chaotic process. All the transitions in thinking that have been described are happening just when adolescent identity formation is becoming a primary task for the young teenager. The "Who am I?" question is consuming for most early adolescents. The urgent need to individuate from family of origin relationships makes it important for adolescents to establish themselves as individuals, each with his or her own unique identity.

If you've been tracking with me and putting all the pieces of this complicated cognitive puzzle together, you can probably see where I'm going with this. The young adolescent has the cognitive ability to look back on 12 or 13 years of "isolated consecutive events" and integrate those events into a personal story. Often, negative themes begin to emerge in these stories—such as abandonment, betrayal, isolation, inadequacy, fear, or defectiveness.

All this is happening at this time when the identity question looms largest. "Who am I?" one adolescent might say. "Well, let me think about that for a minute. When I was little, my dad was never there for me...My teacher told me I was stupid...I was always picked last for the team...I got bullied on the playground... My mom drank too much...I was sexually abused by a babysitter I should've been able to trust..." This process leads many adolescents to significantly distorted conclusions as they attempt to establish a personal identity. "I'll tell you who I am!...I'm a loser...I'm unlovable...I'm incapable of healthy intimacy...I'm unworthy...I'm stupid...I'm disgusting."

Perhaps the best way to describe these conclusions is to call them unchallenged assumptions. The emerging adolescent mind summarizes and interprets personal history and arrives at conclusions often expressed in terms of personal identity. Because of the absence of objective and loving adults in the lives of many adolescents, these assumptions are rarely challenged. In fact, my experience is that adolescents often cling tenaciously to these assumptions because they provide a way to make sense out of past events. Listen to Mandy's painful explanation of all this:

> *Life works for me as long as I view myself as a worthless piece of crap. I am useless, I am nothing. I am unlovable, and that's why my mom drank when I was little. I am a whore so I was sexually abused when I was seven. I am a slut which is why I was raped when I was 13.*

The words Mandy uses to describe herself are assumptions she makes based on her interpretation of what's happened to her during her life. If these words are true—if she can actually persuade herself that she's useless, a slut, a piece of crap—then everything makes sense. In her mind these intensely negative words describe her identity perfectly. It's no wonder she routinely assaults her body. The disdain she feels for herself makes cutting and burning herself a perfectly understandable response.

For some young people the assumptions are expressed visually. Listen to Kerry's vivid description of how he pictures his true identity:

> *I am a rag! I'm a rag covered in vomit and blood and semen. No one may touch this disgusting rag or they too will become filthy and contaminated. Rags get thrown away when people*

are done with them or they become so dirty that they're of no value anymore. I hope that's what happens to me because that's what I deserve. Everyone get out of my life—just leave me alone.

The intense visual image was taken from Kerry's journal. The dirty rag metaphor offered him the words to express his understanding of events that had happened to him, making complete sense of his past.

A HINT FOR HELPERS

It's worth recognizing that we all live with unchallenged assumptions in our lives. Even as an adult, I know that much of who I am today has been shaped by how I saw myself when I was a teenager. What are some unchallenged assumptions you have brought with you into adulthood? As we recognize our tendency to be driven by some of our own distorted thinking, we'll be more insightful and compassionate as we help kids sort through their unchallenged assumptions.

When "Unloved" Becomes "Unlovable"

There is one related observation that might be worth noting as we discuss these assumptions kids make about who they are. Consider the difference between a kid who feels "unloved" and the one who feels "unlovable." The former speaks about an emotion that is being felt at a particular moment, while the latter suggests a deeply rooted sense of negative identity. "Unlovable" says something about who I am, not simply what's going on in my life right now.

Perhaps this distinction sheds a little light on the concept of shame, which is such a large part of the thinking of many hurting kids. We'll discuss this more thoroughly in a later chapter, but for now understand that in the mind of a teenager, shame equals personal defectiveness. Whereas guilt is rooted in something I've done, shame is based in who I am. The despair and hopelessness that come from believing oneself to be "unlovable" make the grip of behaviors like self-injury that much more difficult to break.

It's a daunting task to try to persuade teenagers like Mandy and Kerry that they are precious, respected, deeply valued, and loved by God. Even if they accept these things as theologically true, the fear of embracing this truth about their own identities is greater than many kids can handle. For kids like this, beginning to believe they are beautiful or lovable or worthy of relationship raises a whole other set of questions centering on one word: "Why?" Believing something more positive about themselves takes away their explanation for why these painful things have happened to them. As long as the negative self-images remain in place, all they have to do is find ways to compensate for their flaws and camouflage their weaknesses or—as we see in the case of kids who self-injure—turn their self-contempt inward and vent their emotions through their self-inflicted wounds.

AM I TALKING TO YOU?

What do you see when you look in the mirror? Take a moment right now to review some of the words you've used to describe yourself, and some of the pictures that help you define who you are. If these words and pictures are mostly negative, ask yourself where those ideas came from. As you begin to make those connections, I want to challenge you to talk to someone who can help you sort the truth from the lies. My guess is that most of your negative self-talk is not true.

Challenging the Assumptions

One of the opportunities we have as those who are committed to loving and encouraging self-injurers is to intentionally and thoughtfully challenge the distorted and negative assumptions they've made about themselves. But this might represent a bigger job than we first realize.

Even though many kids find ways to express these assumptions verbally or in writing through words and images, they generally don't respond well to having their assumptions challenged by words alone. Simply telling a deeply wounded, shame-driven teenager she or he is awesome, enjoyable, significant, or loved may not be enough. I believe this is because those negative assumptions are held in a much deeper place in the soul. Because they were most often generated in disappointing relationships, they need to be challenged through loving, consistent, committed relationships. It's not that words have no value, but words that aren't backed up by relationship may seem bleak and hollow to a wounded heart. We'll talk later in the book about what it means to offer that kind of caring relationship to a kid who cuts.

Ultimately, the most effective way we can respond to kids who have such distorted assumptions about their own identities is to help them discover and then embrace the truth of their identity in Christ. The Scripture is full of vivid pictures describing who we are in relationship with him. Children of God (Galatians 4:7). God's sons and daughters (2 Corinthians 6:18). Royalty (1 Peter 2:9). A new creation (2 Corinthians 5:17). The list goes on and on.

At the beginning of this chapter you read the familiar words from Romans 12:2 "be transformed by the renewing of your mind." For kids who cut, that transformation means they learn to believe what God says about them rather than what they have concluded about themselves. This will inevitably mean laying aside the distorted interpretations and assumptions that seemed to make sense of confusing events and painful circumstances. The risks in that will be immense, because giving up those assumptions will, in some significant ways, mean giving up control. As we explore more deeply the motivations behind self-injurious behavior, we'll discover that control is a central theme—controlling pain, controlling how people see me, controlling relationships, controlling the future, and controlling my own body.

Wouldn't it be nice if self-injury were just a random behavior and we could help simply by telling people to stop? Obviously, it's a whole lot more tangled than that, and any real long-term solutions will require more than just a change in behavior.

Now that we understand a little more about the way a hurting kid's mind works, let's take another look at why self-injury is the solution of choice for so many kids.

THE $1,000,000 QUESTION: WHY?

CHAPTER 7

"Cutting is not attention seeking. It is not manipulative. It is a coping mechanism—a punitive, unpleasant, potentially danger- ous one—but it works, it helps me cope with strong emotions that I don't know how to deal with. Don't tell me I'm sick, don't tell me to stop. Don't try to make me feel guilty, that's how I feel already. Listen to me, support me, help me."

Andrew, as quoted in Marilee Strong's *A Bright Red Scream*

It should be clear by now that self-injury is deeply linked to emo- tional and relational pain. Unfortunately, that alone doesn't answer the question of why some people choose to harm themselves as a response to what's happening in their lives. We know there are many ways to deal with personal pain. Some are healthy, others are less so, and still others are, quite frankly, highly dysfunctional and relationally destructive. Self-injury falls into that last cate- gory. The cost is immense—far more than a teenager is capable of understanding. But in moments of immense pain, loneliness, and confusion, it seems to the struggling youth that the gain will out-weigh the loss. And most cutters will tell you that, in terms of reliev-ing immediate pain in the moment, self-injury actually works.

The Price Isn't Right

Before we try to understand the powerful reasoning that drives this behavior, let's take a look at the high price that self-injurers must pay in order to receive the "benefits" self-injury can theo-retically deliver. The costs are both personal and relational.

Perhaps the most obvious cost is seen in the physical dam-age done to the body of the self-injurer. I think of Tonya, a col-lege freshman who came to talk with me the morning after a particularly severe cutting episode. She'd had no choice but to go to the emergency room for treatment. On each of her arms were five deep cuts, each at least two inches long, all spaced perfectly evenly between her wrist and her shoulder. Each cut had been stitched shut with 6 neat sutures—60 stitches in all. In spite of the doctor's careful and skilled attention, those scars will be a lifelong reminder of a desperately painful adolescence.

A HINT FOR HELPERS

Undoubtedly, you've already gained a sense of how fragile your relation-ship with a self-injurer can be. Many of them have experienced more than their share of rejection and abandonment. When a young person chooses to share their deep pain with you, you have the opportunity to model what a trustworthy relationship can feel like. Hang in there with that kid—estab-lish appropriate boundaries so your own life remains healthy, but show that young person what it means to have someone who truly cares. It may be the most significant gift you can offer a kid who cuts.

Even a normal everyday activity like shopping for clothes holds little pleasure because every wardrobe decision must be considered in light of what it will reveal to people. Swimming, suntanning, working out, playing sports—these are all problems unless the self-injurer is willing to let the whole world in on the secret. A college student I worked with recently had to forego being in her best friend's wedding because the bridesmaid dresses were sleeveless; she simply was not prepared to show anyone the damage. In her words, "If I let them see my arms, I've let them see my heart...and nobody gets to see my heart."

And what about the relational cost? Teenagers can be brutally cruel to one another. School is often a dangerous place for self-injurers. They become the butt of jokes and the subject of whispered speculation and rumors, generally feeling like they are on the outside looking in. They may be viewed as freaks and misfits and will likely be treated as though they are. Perhaps this is one reason why in recent years we have seen small "tribes" of self-injurers emerging on high school and college campuses. They eat together, hang out together after classes, and may even meet regularly to compare cuts from the night before. Sometime kids who self-injure gather together for group cutting sessions—a sort of bizarre communion ritual where like-minded kids can get just a little taste of community. What was once a lonely and secret activity becomes a point of camaraderie and connection. Sadly, they are bound together primarily by the brokenness they share.

It nearly goes without saying that dating and ultimately marriage represent huge risks. Many of the self-injurers I've met (especially girls) believe they have disqualified themselves permanently from that sort of intimate relationship. My observation is that those self-injurers who do open themselves to dating relationships often land in twisted, dysfunctional ones. Their own self-contempt keeps them from pursuing relationships with people who are healthier, because they believe no one whose life is on track would ever be attracted to them.

Even those self-injurers who find a trusting love relationship know their past actions will have a lasting effect. Adrian is a handsome young man in his mid-20s who is well established in a job. I got to know Adrian and his fiancée last year, when I was doing their premarital counseling. During one of those sessions Adrian rolled up his sleeve to show me an arm covered with hundreds of scars. Through tears he apologized to his fiancée for the damage she would now have to live with for the rest of her life. She gently and freely forgave him, but I could see in her eyes that she knew she was being asked to pay a price as well.

For many self-injurers the sense of personal defectiveness that motivated their cutting is reinforced by the undeniable physical evidence of being flawed. In many cases this turns into a shame-driven cycle where the motivation to stop is diminished by a feeling of hopeless despair that grows with each successive episode.

Beneath all this for most self-injurers is the helpless feeling that life is out of control. I've yet to meet a self-injurer who actually believes this coping mechanism is healthy or appropriate. Most self-injurers desperately want to stop but are terrified to do so. In chapter 9 we'll look in more detail at why cutters find it so hard to quit—but suffice it to say the tug-of-war between knowing they must stop and the fear associated with that decision creates an ongoing feeling of emotional chaos.

Listen to the poem 16-year-old Sara wrote to express the tension she feels as she weighs the pros and cons of giving in to the powerful pull of self-injury. The despair is palpable, and the poem may seem almost like a suicide note—but in fact it is the desperate cry of a self-injurer who goes through this agonizing process over and over each time her emotions become unbearable.

Everyday I wake up hoping to die, but truly all I
can really do is cry.
The little voice inside says "grab the knife and
do it!"

But my friends would never let me go through it.
You can't hold the feeling inside any longer,
You grab the knife and start to ponder.
As you sit there on the bathroom floor,
You wait and wait and wait some more.
Finally, you put the knife to your wrist,
As you clench the memories in your fist.
"Do it, Do it" is all you hear, you feel a little
pinch of fear.
You slide the knife across your wrist,
Little by little the memories will leave your fist.
You're almost done, you'll end being no one.
There you've done it, you fought that battle of
fear and won.
It's over now there is no more,
As you lie there on the blood-covered floor.

The pain I feel as I read these words gives me a small sense of just how difficult it is for a teenager who self-injures to break the cycle. The release Sara feels is almost tangible as she says, "There you've done it, you fought that battle of fear and won." But the sad truth is that the relief she feels is only temporary—the personal ache will return. Sarah's honest words express the tension that millions of young people feel on a regular basis as they struggle to decide if and when they'll turn to the blade again.

Shouldn't Church Make It Easier?

Those of us in the church need to be aware that Christian kids who self-injure struggle with issues that may only intensify their suffering. Many such kids feel an overwhelming sense of guilt because of their apparent inability to appropriate God's healing power. It seems God is able to help everyone else be victorious, but their only experience is a string of failures. They hear Scripture verses about God's desire to transform people, but these verses don't seem to apply to their situations. Here's how Mike describes the feeling:

> I look around me during the worship time at youth group. Everyone seems so into it with their hands raised and big smiles on their faces. I couldn't raise my hands even if I felt like it, cuz then everybody'd just be staring at my ugly arms. We sing songs about how God can take away our pain and heal our hurts, but my guess is that not one of those goody-goodies has ever had any real pain or hurt in their life.

Add to that guilt and alienation the inability of many churches to respond appropriately to self-injuring behavior, and you're left with a group of believers who are desperately lonely in their pain. Too many churches are places where people feel they must put on their happiest face in order to feel like they belong. Self-injurers may try their best to show everyone that everything is okay, but the overwhelming nature of their struggle makes it difficult for them to maintain the façade for long. They end up believing (perhaps with good reason) that if people knew who they really were, they'd be ostracized like the lepers of Bible times.

Guilt, shame, fear, loneliness, alienation, ridicule, an uncertain future, an unbearable present, and a past that keeps rearing its ugly head—the cost of self-injury is undeniably high. Yet in their deeply hurting hearts, many kids believe their reasons for doing it are worth the price they must pay.

A HINT FOR HELPERS

Adults working with young people should ask themselves, "How safe are kids in the groups we lead? Have we established ground rules for healthy relationships? Are we taking appropriate steps to eliminate bullying, exclusivity, and inappropriate social stratification? Does everyone feel safe in the relational communities we are inviting them to join?

I Cut to Make Things Better

The answers self-injurers give to the "Why?" question are widely varied. In fact, as I've listened to the stories of countless individuals over the years, each one is driven by a unique combination of factors. No two kids are alike, so every situation involves listening carefully to the story and then helping the youth determine her or his specific reasons for self-injuring.

The reasons tend to cluster under a half-dozen broad themes we'll explore together in these next pages. But in different ways, each of them must be understood as a strategy for self-care rather than as a means of self-harm.

Most kids who cut feel that life actually improves after an episode of self-injury. This is one reason they struggle with terms like self-harm or self-mutilation. In a profound understatement, 16-year-old Leslie summarizes what most people don't understand about kids who hurt themselves: *"I cut to make things better..."*

In order to help the teenager who self-injures, you must understand this fundamental motivation. The truth is that the things most cutters long for are completely legitimate. It's not inappropriate for kids to want committed adults richly involved in their lives. It's completely understandable for kids to look for ways to manage emotions that feel out of control. It's not wrong to long to be loved, to belong, to know you're safe, or to feel comfortable with your gender or sexuality. The desires are reasonable and good and should be affirmed as such.

Let's have a closer look at some specific reasons kids give for harming themselves.

"I need to feel SOMETHING!"

A lot of kids who resort to self-injury tell me that much of the time they feel nothing at all. They describe their lives as emotionally empty or numb. This absence of affect creates a feeling of deadness and is intensely unsettling. Kids talk about feeling hollow or being spectators to their own lives. They often report that everything around them feels surreal, as if they're actually not participating in what's happening around them.

A physical cut or burn that produces actual, tangible pain is a way of reconnecting to reality. The fact that they wince and that their blood flows reminds them they are still alive—in spite of how they feel most of the time. Vince describes the feeling with a pretty vivid image:

> For me life is often like seeing myself in an old black-and-white movie. It's dingy and gray. I watch myself going through the motions of my day—school, home, practice, work—and I don't feel a thing. But then when I cut I see the red. It's the only color on the screen and it reminds me that I'm not just a spectator to this boring bland picture show.

What would cause someone to feel numb, dead, and emotionally disconnected from the daily activities surrounding him or her? Perhaps it has to do with how these kids have learned to deal with their emotions up to this point in their lives.

The human capacity for emotional range is astounding. It extends from the deepest agony in the midst of grief and loss to the most intense elation and ecstasy when life is filled with joy and satisfaction. We were meant to live on that continuum, experiencing the full range of these feelings in ways appropriate to our circumstances at any given moment.

When kids live with an inordinate amount of pain, they often find ways to camouflage, stuff, or ignore the negative emotions. Unfortunately, the only way they can diminish sensitivity to negative feelings is by becoming numb to their overall emotional state. But as they intentionally limit the negative emotions they allow themselves to feel, they inadvertently shut down the positive as well. Emotional denial results in numbness at both ends of the spectrum. There is less pain and sadness, but the capacity for laughter and delight is also lost. Life turns gray.

There's another reason some kids are numb to their emotions and tend to experience life more as spectator than participant. It's especially common among kids who have had an unusually traumatic childhood. When one experiences high levels of anxiety, fear, uncertainty, and confusion, the body is kept in a constant state of stress. Muscles stay taut, adrenaline flows, sleep patterns are interrupted, and the mind is always active—constantly remaining "on guard." For kids in traumatic situations, this crisis state eventually begins to feel like a normal emotional baseline. Self-injuring behavior creates an artificial crisis—which feels normal to such kids. Anything less feels like emotional deadness. The only way they can feel alive is by re-creating their own trauma, thus returning to what in their minds feels like "life as it should be."

"I'm bad and I deserve to be punished!"

The belief that he or she is inherently bad is one of the most consuming conclusions a young adolescent can come to. It's a perfect example of one of those "unchallenged assumptions" we talked about earlier. Even though we may do all we can to persuade a young person this is not the case, this mindset is often an extremely difficult one to break.

Kids get the message they are bad in a variety of ways. It may be as simple as careless parents who have constantly reminded their children of their inadequacies and failures. "You're a bad boy!" "That's something only a bad girl would do!" Unfortunately, at some point kids have no choice but to believe what they've always been told. (Remember what we said earlier about how adolescents use information from their pasts as they try to craft a personal identity.) Many of them come from homes that are also lacking in love and spontaneous affection. That absence of nurture, combined with ubiquitous reminders of failure, can combine to give kids an overwhelming sense of personal defectiveness. These family environments speak two powerful messages to the sensitive heart of a child: "You are a failure and a disappointment" and "I don't love you." Many kids conclude that the reason they aren't loved is because they're a failure. It's not hard to understand how "being bad" would be at the heart of their personal identities.

Other kids have a belief that they need to be punished that is rooted in more specific events or relationships. Victims of abuse often mistakenly believe those terrible things happened to them because they were bad. Vicki was sexually abused by an older brother for almost seven years, and then was called a liar when she finally had the courage to tell her parents. She asks a series of questions that give us a sense of what this feels like:

> What makes me think I deserve anything better than what I'm getting right now? Why would anyone in their right mind want anything to do with me? Why would God ever forgive someone as evil as I am? Why the hell did he bring me into this world if he knew this would happen? How will I survive in this life knowing that my insides are black, my heart is disgusting, I can never come clean? Don't try to tell me I'm not bad! Don't try to love me. I know the truth.

Now, add to this painful past the guilt associated with self-injury, and the cycle of self-contempt is not hard to understand. When kids believe they are bad, it is much more difficult for them to create boundaries that will keep them from other destructive behaviors. Perhaps this is one reason why so many kids who self-injure also abuse alcohol, dabble in drugs, participate in sexually inappropriate behavior, and develop other destructive habits—all of which come back to remind them they really are bad.

"Would someone please notice me?"

We were created for relationship. As human beings, we long to share our journey with other people. The desire to know and be known by others is fundamental to our existence. We simply cannot live healthy lives in isolation. The desire for relational connectedness and belonging seems particularly intense during adolescence. As kids begin to disengage from their families of origin, they seek new places to connect both with their peers and with significant nonparental adults.

Kids long to stand out from the crowd and will sometimes go to extreme measures to accomplish that goal. One way to distinguish themselves from all the others around them is to present a need that urgently begs for a response. Self-injury is the perfect solution for some young people. It shouts, "I'm different! I'm unique! I'm desperately needy!" Of course, when others' involvement in their lives is generated in response to self-injury, kids eventually come to believe that such crises are the only way to invite others into relationship. They fear that if they "get better," there'll be no reason for anyone to remain in relationship with them.

AM I TALKING TO YOU?

Can you imagine the joy of a relationship that is truly mutual? I'm talking about a relationship in which you don't *have* to do anything to keep going. No need to demand or manipulate. No need to be needy. Try to develop those kinds of relationships with some of the people around you whom you've learned to trust. Look for ways you can invite them into your life by honestly asking for their help, instead of feeling like you need to pressure them to be there for you.

At the beginning of the book, I introduced you to Kelly and her painfully lonely circumstances. Just a few days ago I was having lunch with her near her school, and in the midst of a conversation she blurted out a random question: "What happens to us when I stop cutting? I'll still need you sometimes, you know. Will you still want to spend time with me when I'm not cutting anymore?" One way Kelly has been able to get many adults involved in her life is by communicating the message that she can't survive without them. Her fear of losing that point of connection is almost enough to keep her in her self-harming cycle.

For many kids, fresh injuries are a tangible means of validating the depth of pain they are feeling. "You want to know how badly I hurt? Just have a look at this!" Fourteen-year-old Rachel used her freshly injured arms in a desperate attempt to get her dad to pay some attention. He was starting a new business while continuing to work his day job, and in the process he disappeared from her life. He told me his wake-up call came one night when his young daughter walked into his home office in her pajamas to say "good night." As she reached out to hug him, drops of blood fell from her freshly wounded arms onto the papers he was working on. When he frantically asked her what had happened, she nonchalantly replied, "It's just what I do when I miss you."

"Would everyone please leave me alone!"

As much as some kids use self-injury as a way of getting people to come close, others use it to accomplish just the opposite. Some adolescents have become so weary and wounded in their attempts to invite involvement from the people around them that they've given up. They have tried to get attention from parents, teachers, coaches, and perhaps even therapists (I'm amazed at the number of kids for whom I am their third or sixth or tenth counselor), but all they've received is more rejection. At some point it becomes too painful to keep allowing people to get close. When that happens, it's as if a switch has been flipped. Instead of begging people to pay attention, these kids now devote all their energy to pushing people away.

Of course, at the heart of these efforts to keep people away is a deep fear. It's the fear of being disappointed again, the fear of becoming dependent on someone and then being abandoned, the fear of learning to enjoy something and then having it taken away. These kids live by the distorted logic that it's better never to hope for anything than to have that hope shattered.

There's not much that pushes people away more quickly than a fresh cut or two amidst a sea of scars. Most people find themselves recoiling in horror or shock. For the self-injurer who wants to keep people at a distance, this is mission accomplished. But it's important to remember that, even though these kids use their wounds as a way of keeping people away, behind that callused front is a lonely, broken heart desperately longing for love.

It can be tremendously difficult to continually reach out to a kid who pushes people away, but gentle perseverance pays huge dividends. Having said that, I must remind you that if you choose to move toward a kid whose *modus operandi* is to push people away, you'd better pack a lunch—because you have to stay in it for the long haul. To begin building relationships with such kids and then run out when the going gets tough will powerfully reinforce their belief that they are unlovable and make it even more difficult for the future helpers who want to come alongside.

A HINT FOR HELPERS

It's not easy working with kids who reject and abuse those who try to help them. Not everyone can live with the lack of affirmation one often gets in relationships with these kinds of kids. If you are able to find satisfaction in working with hurting kids, let me encourage you to recognize the special gift God has given you. Don't take for granted the love you have for this special group of teenagers. Find ways to continue moving toward them. Chances are there won't be a lot of other adults in their lives. What you have to offer them is a rare and important thing.

"The emotional pressure's more than I can handle!"

After hearing the stories of dozens of kids in my office and reading countless others in online journals and blogs, I have found that one motivation for cutting looms larger than the rest. It shows up at some level in virtually every self-injurer's account of what cutting does for him or her. Each kid seems to have a different way of describing it, but at its core, cutting is simply a pressure relief valve. Listen to Caitlin talk about how it works for her:

> I do it because I can't get mad at people, at least on the surface. Anytime someone acts mean to me or anything, I just get sad. But it all wells up...and then all of a sudden I just sorta snap. Then I run upstairs as fast as I can and cut until everything goes away.

It's not unusual to hear kids talking about a number of reasons that drive their behavior, depending on what's going on in their lives at any given time. Paige describes her experience like this:

> Sometimes I do it just to see my blood and know that I am still alive. Other times I do it to relieve the pressure and desperation that build up inside. The sense of emotional relief after a cut is overwhelming. And scary!

Paige apparently swings back and forth between times she feels emotionally dead and times her emotions are so intense they must be relieved immediately. Notice the comment at the end about how scary it is after she cuts, which gives a sense of how emotionally astute she actually is. Obviously she has an acute awareness of just how powerful this coping technique actually is.

The emotions of even the healthiest adolescents are often intense, chaotic, and pretty close to the surface. Learning to manage those emotions is one of the challenges of becoming an adult. Some kids are privileged to be in relationships where they see healthy emotional management modeled for them regularly. Others are left to figure it out on their own, to find for themselves something that works. When feelings—especially negative ones—become uncontrollable and overwhelming, it can feel like drowning. I've often heard kids say there is nothing they can do to change the emotional pain they find themselves in other than to impose physical pain, which, at least for a moment, will trump that emotional pain.

Sandy is an attractive, outgoing college freshman whose story of sexual abuse and family dysfunction is as severe as any I've ever heard. There is no one in her world she can count on. With the exception of the youth group she was a part of the last few years of high school, she's been surrounded by nothing but abuse. Even her early dating experiences as a preteen involved abusive relationships with older guys. She lives with an overwhelming amount of guilt and shame. Most days she believes there is nothing that can ever be done to heal the pain she feels inside. But she says that watching her body heal after she has cut gives her the smallest glimmer of hope that she may be capable of healing:

> The wound is right there on my arm—I can see it—I can touch it. Unlike the deeper pain that can't be seen, what I did last week is here as visible evidence. I am fascinated as I watch the scab form and then gradually disappear leaving only a thin white reminder of where it hurt a long time ago. Wouldn't it be sweet if my heart healed as easily as my skin?

Whether it's sadness, anger, fear, anxiety, depression, or any of a thousand other painful emotions, many self-injurers have found that the simplest solution is to let it all out through a self-inflicted wound. An online blogger who identifies herself simply as H says it this way:

Drops of blood are my tear drops—when I'm not allowed to cry my body cries for me.

"This actually gives me a buzz."

The human body is a marvel. Our ability to adapt and respond to what is going on around us and what happens to us is astounding. Only in recent years have researchers begun to understand the complex chemical and neurological balances that exist. When the body is injured, it immediately kicks into response mode. Whack your thumb with a hammer and here's what happens: Involuntary responses immediately take over, protecting the body from further hurt, rushing healing agents to the source of the pain through the circulatory system, and adjusting brain chemistry to make the pain bearable. The same is true when a self-injurer puts blade to skin. The resulting buzz may actually be physiologically enjoyable—especially for people who haven't experienced a lot of pleasure in their lives.

There's still a great deal more to be learned about this component of the self-injurious cycle, but it certainly could be part of the motivation for some people. This might be especially true for teenagers who, because of a traumatic or abusive past, can no longer distinguish between pleasure and pain. It is quite common for people who have been sexually abused to mix up the two in their state of emotional confusion. Pleasure actually feels painful, and pain feels pleasant. Untangling this confusion is one of the greatest challenges in helping some self-injurers come to terms with a wound-free future.

I often see kids just a few hours after they've cut. I ask the students I'm counseling to stop by the office for a quick conversation as soon as possible after an episode. For those I'm working with regularly, it's a means of accountability, a reinforcement of the notion that I don't find them repulsive, and an opportunity for me to assess their need for medical attention. I'm amazed that they often describe what happened as "feeling good." I was talking with one of my young self-injuring friends just yesterday. She hasn't cut in more than six weeks, and the tug-of-war going on inside her is unbearable. "It would feel soooooo good!" she begs me, as if she hopes to get my permission to go ahead with it. Once again I am reminded that, on some level I can't understand personally, cutting generates feelings of well-being, calm, control, and relief. It hurts real good.

"I hate being a girl."

There is a small group within the self-injuring community for whom extreme self-contempt is related directly to gender and sexuality. I've gotten to know a number of self-injuring girls whose pain is linked to specific experiences of sexual abuse. In their minds, being female is what actually got them their pain in the first place and they feel an intense anger and disdain for everything that represents their gender identity. (In my experience this is much more common among girls. There is so much more to be learned about the specific ways self-injury functions among guys.) The violence these young women turn toward themselves might probably be called self-mutilation, because the targets of attack are the breasts, genitals, or even the face.

In his excellent book on issues of sexual abuse, *The Wounded Heart,* Dan Allender makes an interesting connection between shame and contempt. He suggests that when persons are filled with intense feelings of shame, they may mistakenly believe the only way to move forward is in a spirit of contempt. Sometimes the contempt is directed toward others, and sometimes it is directed inward. The self-contempt many cutters feel finds expression when they self-injure. In cutting, their self-directed anger finds tangible outlet, and the pressure it produces can be marginally reduced—for a little while at least.

For most adolescents issues of sexuality represent an area of real fragility and vulnerability. Even without a history of abuse, coming to terms with a changing body is one of the major challenges for most adolescents. As kids constantly compare themselves with their peers and with the body-shape role models on magazine covers, feelings of failure and inadequacy can loom large. Knowing that one's body doesn't meet the standard our culture associates with beauty may be enough to start the cycle of self-hatred. When that changing body has been the target of abuse, particularly when the abuse has come from someone who should have been trustworthy, the ensuing shame can be crippling.

As I reconsider some of the reasons teenagers engage in self-injury, I am once again struck by the fact that the motivations are, for the most part, completely legitimate. The desire for relational involvement is one of the core thirsts God placed within every human being. The fear of being hurt again and again when that's been the pattern in one's personal history is certainly understandable. When abuse has occurred, the vulnerability one might feel around gender and sexuality and the desire to defend against further violations are quite reasonable. And we can all relate to the desire to have a measure of control in times of intense emotional chaos.

My point is this: The problem with self-injury is typically not evident in the motivations that drive it. One of the most important things we can do as we journey alongside kids who cut is to affirm the hopes and desires that lead to their behavior, while challenging the reasoning that concludes that harming themselves is the best strategy for accomplishing those outcomes.

HURTS SO BAD: THE PAIN THAT DRIVES SELF-INJURY

CHAPTER 8

"if someone makes me sad...i reach for the razor
if someone makes me angry...i reach for the razor
if someone makes me cry...i reach for the razor
if someone makes me remember...i reach for the razor
if someone makes me see who i am...i reach for the razor
the razor is my road to solitude and happiness...
if only for a little while—it's something..."

Rachel, age 17

It should be abundantly clear by now that there's a strong link between self-injury and personal pain. As we seek to respond more appropriately to that pain, we would do well to explore more deeply the source of all that hurt. Let's start by doing some theological reflection.

Let's Go Back to the Garden

You might be surprised to hear me suggest it all begins with the way we were created. God intended for us to be a whole lot more than physical bodies occupying a few square feet here on earth. The Scriptures clearly illustrate that God's desire was for relationship with his creation. From the beginning of the story, where we find the Creator showing up in the garden during the evening just to hang out with Adam and Eve, to the very end, where we read of God's plan to spend eternity with us—the themes of intimacy and relationship tie the whole Bible together. The essence of sin is that our relationship with God has been broken; the good news of the gospel is that God has initiated a way for relationship to be restored. Throughout the Old Testament God routinely shows up to be present with his people—sometimes in the form of smoke and fire and sometimes in a still small voice. The New Testament carries the theme forward. In Jesus, the Word became flesh and dwelt among us. And as Jesus sits with his disciples in that upper room just hours before his arrest, he assures them they will not be left alone— he will send his Holy Spirit to dwell within them and all who believe. God's desire to be relationally intimate with us is clearly evident throughout Scripture.

But we were not created only for intimacy with God. He designed us for relationship with one another as well. His assessment after creating Adam was that it was "not good" for him to be alone. God created a companion for Adam, and the human race was the result. God's intention was that human relationships would be rich and satisfying. They would be places where individuals were affirmed and valued, places where love could be given joyfully and received freely. The balance demonstrated in God's plan is astounding in its perfection. The deepest thirsts of the human soul would be quenched in a relationship of unhindered intimacy with the Creator. There, truly unconditional love would be freely available. There, a sense of eternal significance and purpose would be found. And our need for belonging would be met as part of his eternal family. The rich satisfaction that flowed from this intimate relationship with God would express itself in healthy relationships between people. Because our deepest thirsts were being met in relationship with God, we wouldn't need to demand from one another what was already freely available from God. Sounds good, doesn't it?

A HINT FOR HELPERS

I'm sure it's obvious by now that this resource is written from a "faith-based" point of view. If you don't share that perspective, some of the language in this section may be foreign to you. Nonetheless, I'd encourage you to keep reading. I believe that spiritual solutions are a critical part of complete hope and healing. I've found that the most comprehensive path to wholeness involves an engagement with spiritual truth. I'd invite you to consider what's here as a way of appropriating such truth.

Every human being who has ever walked the earth from Adam and Eve's day to our own has lived a deep longing that can be truly satisfied only in a relationship of authentic intimacy with God. But the first humans weren't in the garden for long before the story takes a bad turn. You're probably familiar with it. One day Eve finds herself in conversation with a sly and beguiling serpent. He paints God as a cosmic spoilsport who wants to make life miserable by imposing unreasonable restrictions and unfair rules. The serpent suggests that if Adam and Eve really want to experience life in its fullest, they just need to declare their independence by stepping over the line God has drawn in the sand and showing they aren't going to live by his rules any longer. Obviously, this sounds reasonable to Eve, and before long she and Adam are biting into that apple. They could never have imagined how immense the implications would be.

But what does any of this have to do with self-injury? Don't worry—I haven't forgotten what this book is about. You see, every teenager you and I know was born with the same deep longings Adam and Eve were seeking to satisfy. And like Adam and Eve, when they try to find ways to satisfy those longings apart from God, the result is disappointment and self-doubt.

The most common metaphor used in Scripture to describe these longings is thirst. Psalm 42 begins, "As the deer pants for streams of water, so my soul pants for you, my God. My soul thirsts for God, for the living God" (vv.1-2). Isaiah exuberantly invites God's people to experience a fully thirst-quenching banquet in Isaiah 55: "Come, all you who are thirsty, come to the waters; and you who have no money, come, buy and eat! Come, buy wine and milk without money and without cost" (v. 1).

Jesus picks up the same theme in John 4 when he bumps into a Samaritan woman at a well one day. She's tried relationships with many men and has found them all dissatisfying for one reason or another. Recognizing a deep thirst in her that wouldn't be quenched by another five husbands or a thousand buckets of water, Jesus offers her the "living water" that will truly quench her thirst.

God's original plan was that our deep thirst would be fully sated in our relationship with him. But when he is written out of the equation, our only option is to look to our circumstances or to one another as the means for quenching that thirst. Yet everything short of God leaves us dissatisfied and disappointed.

Let's look more specifically at three areas of thirst, or longing, we'll find in the soul of every teenager:

Just Love Me...Please

First off, every kid longs to be loved with no conditions. Unfortunately, in our performance-based culture, it's often more about what they do than who they are. Academic achievement, athletic success, physical attractiveness, and other external measures are often the basis upon which kids feel either loved or rejected. To be deeply loved simply for who they are is something many kids can only dream of.

God's love is unconditional, and he promises to quench the deepest thirst. In one of Scripture's many lavish expressions of God's unfailing love, the prophet Jeremiah voices God's encouraging words to his beleaguered people: "I have loved you with an everlasting love; I have drawn you with unfailing kindness. I will build you up again" (Jeremiah 31:3-4). What a significant look at God's heart for stressed and struggling kids who thirst for that kind of love.

Does My Life Matter?

Secondly, all teenagers feel a deep longing to know that their lives have significance and purpose. The desire to feel they are actually making a difference gives them a sense of worth and value. Most kids I know feel there aren't many adults who take them seriously most of the time. Maybe we refer to teenagers as "the church of tomorrow," but the programs we design often seem designed to entertain rather than empower them. Adolescents are wired for adventure, purpose, and passion, yet they often find themselves boxed in, restricted, and prevented from dreaming about what their generation could accomplish.

A POINT FOR PARENTS

It's important for us to recognize our role in giving our sons and daughters an appropriate feeling of significance. We can't just tell them they matter—we need to show through our actions and attitudes that we value their opinions and respect their thoughts. The way we relate to our kids will communicate how much we value our relationships with them. Every kid will try to find a way to be significant. Some find ways that reflect maturity and balance, while others find destructive and ineffective ways to make an impact. Let's help our kids feel a healthy sense of significance instead of leaving them on their own to find ways to quench this thirst.

God's plan was that a young person's thirst for significance would be fully satisfied in the pursuit of eternal purposes. Ephesians 2:10 reminds us the teenagers we know are "God's handiwork, created in Christ Jesus to do good works, which God prepared in advance for [them] to do."

The Desire for Belonging

There is a third area of longing, and those of us who spend a lot of time with teenagers don't need to be reminded of what a powerful motivator it is. I'm talking about the thirst for belonging. There is nothing more painful and devastating for most teenagers than to be isolated, to feel like they're on the outside looking in. Walk into any school cafeteria at lunch and look at the kids who are sitting alone. Their faces usually tell the story of what they feel inside. For those of us who care deeply about kids, it's agonizing to see. We've all seen kids who are so desperate to belong that they'll do virtually anything to earn the favor of those who decide whether they're in or not.

Like the previous two components of adolescent thirst, this longing to belong is also meant to be met God's way. Membership in a true community of faith should ensure rich satisfaction in this area. A little further on in Ephesians 2, Paul reminds people that they are "no longer foreigners and strangers, but fellow citizens with God's people and also members of his household" (v. 19). Paul goes on to say that in Christ we "are being built together to become a dwelling in which God lives by his spirit" (v. 23). We were created to belong!

Here is where it all starts to come together. Most of the kids I work with have a painful and deeply rooted disappointment in one or more of these three areas of thirst. They feel unloved, insignificant, and/or relationally isolated. Nearly all the reasons kids give for resorting to self-injurious behavior can be traced back to a deep unsatisfied desire in at least one of these three areas. The unchallenged assumptions we've talked about in earlier chapters are actually expressions of these unquenched thirsts.

"I'm ugly...I'm stupid...I'm unworthy" are all really just expressions of "I'm unlovable."

"I'm nothing...I don't matter...No one cares" are statements that articulate deep feelings of inadequacy and insignificance.

"I'm a dork...I'm a loser...I'm a klutz" are other ways to say, "I don't belong and I probably never will."

Your Fault or Mine?

It's clear a lot of kids who turn to self-injury have deep wounds that were the result of choices others have made. In its simplest terms, these kids hurt *because bad things have happened to them.* We can legitimately call these kids *victims* because the pain they feel is not the result of choices they've made. They are the children of divorce, children of alcoholics, sexual abuse survivors, the abandoned, the neglected, the traumatized. Someone else was responsible for the pain these kids feel.

But most of us are aware of a second category of kids. Much of the pain they live with stems directly from the relational and behavioral decisions they are making. We could accurately say these kids are hurting *because they are making bad choices.* The technical term for these kids is *agents* because in a very real sense they are responsible for the outcomes they live with. These are typically the kids who seem unable to "just say no." They may choose to abuse alcohol or drugs, to live their lives promiscuously (with all the implications that accompany that choice), or to involve themselves with a group of friends who will clearly drag them down. Sometimes, we may look at these kids and shake our heads in disbelief. "How could you have done a stupid thing like that?" we ask. "What did you think would happen next?"

The solution for each of these groups may seem obvious at first. If kids are victims, and their pain is not of their own choosing, then clearly they need support, protection, nurture, and encouragement. We need to walk alongside these kids and let them know they're not alone. We must provide a supportive, loving environment where they can be cared for in safety and begin to grow toward health.

On the other hand, if kids are agents and the pain in their lives is a result of their bad choices, our response seems equally clear. We need to hold them accountable, allow them to live with the consequences of their choices, and challenge them to make wiser decisions in the future. These kids must be told to wise up, stop hurting themselves, and start making better choices about who they hang out with and what they do with their time.

Wouldn't it be nice if it were all this simple? All we'd have to do is determine whether the pain of a young person was connected to their victimization or based in their agency. Once that determination was made, we could respond appropriately with either a timely hug or a well-placed kick in the pants.

The Messy Tangle of Victimization and Agency

The problem, as you probably know, is that it's usually much messier than this. In fact, many self-injuring kids—perhaps even *most* self-injurers—find themselves *making bad choices* BECAUSE *bad things have happened to them.* This creates a whole new set of challenges for us as helpers.

The good news is that the ministry of Jesus provides a wonderful model that can give us some insight into how to respond in these situations. Throughout the Gospels we see Jesus encountering people who seem, on the surface, to fit into these two categories. There were plenty of victims—orphans, widows, lepers, the woman who had been bleeding for 12 years, the lame, the blind—all in pain that apparently had nothing to do with their own choices. But Jesus encountered his share of agents as well—Zacchaeus, the woman at the well (who'd obviously made some ill-informed marital choices), the woman caught in adultery, Peter (who chose poorly more than once), and even the thief on the cross. These people had made devastating choices that were causing them great pain.

In his infinite wisdom Jesus responded to both kinds of people in love and gentleness. His actions toward these people were always filled with compassion and often characterized by an appropriate firmness. In short, *Jesus consistently loved people as they were, but he refused to leave them as they were.* This is what we must seek to do.

When we work with kids who have chosen to self-injure (notice the intentional use of the language of agency) we must recognize that in the vast majority of cases those choices are tangled up with a sad story of victimization. For many kids, the cycle of self-injury begins with an experience of victimization. It could be something major like a family breakdown, or something that might seem minor like being cut from a sports team, dumped by a girlfriend, or left off the guest list for a Saturday night party.

PAINFUL EVENTS
Victimization

Adolescents often misinterpret these events and assume that what has happened is somehow their own fault. They believe the pain is the result of their own defectiveness. And here's where those unchallenged assumptions we talked about earlier begin to emerge. All of the "I am..." statements that allow teenagers to define their own negative identities are embraced.

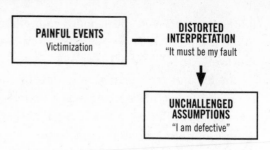

The cycle continues as the victimized young person begins to live out the negative assumptions made. "If I am nothing, if I'm a bag of trash, if I'm a whore...then I know how to live." As I've watched kids come to terms with these negative assumptions, I've seen that their efforts toward survival and self-protection typically take one of three forms:

- *Compensate:* "I must make up for my defectiveness. No one can be allowed to see my ugly insides. I have to find ways to make people love me. I'll ensure that everyone around me is pleased with who I am. As long as no one knows what's really going on inside, I can make myself acceptable."

- *Deny and distract:* "Hurt? I don't know what you're talking about. I feel fine—in fact, I'm having too much fun to worry about what's going on inside. I'll take risks; I'll run on adrenaline; I'll use drugs, alcohol, and sex—whatever it takes to make sure I never have to think about how much I'm hurting. I can't feel a thing, and I like it that way."

- *Express/live out my assumptions:* "I'm a loser, a disappointment, a failure—and that's how I'll choose to live. It's impossible for me to pretend I'm anything else, so I won't even try. Most of the time it leaves me feeling dead inside, but that's probably better than trying to fix something that can never be fixed."

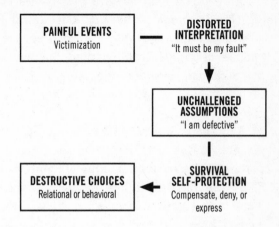

Whether kids choose to compensate for their negative self-images, deny them and distract themselves from facing reality, or express these negative assumptions by living them out, the resulting choices will often be unhealthy and destructive. This leads to increased stress levels, intensified anxiety, and greater guilt. Another probable outcome is a further breakdown in their most important relationships. Kids may pretend everything is okay, but the pain they are living is multiplying to reach a whole new level.

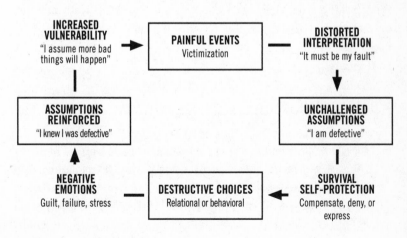

Now the negative assumptions are reinforced. "I really am a loser... I am unlovable... I am repulsive." As these beliefs become more deeply entrenched, the level of vulnerability kids live with increases proportionately. This inevitably sets them up for additional experiences of victimization and sets the cycle spinning again.

What must be understood about this pattern I'm describing is that it doesn't just travel 'round and 'round like an amusement park carousel. In fact, I imagine it more like a tornado, spiraling downward in ever-tighter circles. As the circles shrink, the pace of the whole process quickens. Eventually, two things happen. First, things start to feel completely out of control. Second, and perhaps even more significantly, the circle begins to become restrictive. What was once wide and open with space available for relationships with others becomes cramped, tiny, and claustrophobic, leaving room for only one. The despair of finding oneself in this lonely yet emotionally chaotic space will lead to increasingly desperate measures like self-injury as means of survival.

As those who love and care for kids who hurt themselves, we have the blessed opportunity to live out Christ's love for them. Whether the kids we know are acting out of painful victimization or expressing their agency by making negative choices, we must, like Jesus, love them as they are but refuse to leave them as they are.

A HINT FOR HELPERS

Keep in mind the uncomplicated ways Christ expressed love for the people around him. He spent time hanging out with them, he let them see what was going on in his life, he used teachable moments to communicate truth, and he firmly challenged them when they needed correction and lovingly affirmed them to remind them of their value. We can love kids in the same ways!

The Place of Repentance

Repentance is the appropriate response, regardless of whether one's situation is primarily victimization or agency. In the church we often think of repentance in terms of confessing our own sins, so the word might seem inappropriate in a case of victimization, where another person is the cause of one's suffering. But repentance is better understood as a turning—and not primarily a turning away from sin, but a turning *to Someone*. We've become so accustomed to seeing sin as a behavioral issue rather than a relational one, we tend to define repentance as turning from certain sinful behavior. But at its heart, sin is relational—and so is repentance.

We must invite kids to turn to the loving Father who eagerly awaits the return of his beloved child. This is the call to repentance. As kids turn to the One who loves them perfectly, there will be a natural turning away from choices that are dangerous and destructive. That's where they'll find hope and healing.

A Special Word on Sexual Abuse

Before we close our discussion on sources of pain, it seems important to acknowledge the strong correlation between sexual abuse and self-injury. It is a profoundly devastating experience to have one's sexuality violated, particularly by a trusted person. The deep sense of shame that accompanies almost all memories of sexual abuse is a powerful shaping force in the life of young people and adults who live with it.

In situations of sexual abuse, the body is assaulted but the soul experiences the deepest damage. Everything we've said in this chapter about the relationship between our woundedness and the way we respond to it is multiplied when we're dealing with persons who have experienced sexual abuse. To learn more about the impact of sexual abuse and how survivors can find a path to wholeness, I highly recommend Dr. Dan Allender's *The Wounded Heart*.

One final thought about this topic might be in order. While we know there is a strong correlation between sexual abuse and self-injury, it would be wrong to assume that anyone who self-injures has likely been sexually abused. The pain that leads to self-harm comes in a wide variety of forms and intensities. Let kids tell their stories to you. Listen carefully to what they say, but don't make assumptions based merely on statistics you might have read.

IT JUST HAPPENS: UNDERSTANDING THE CYCLE OF ADDICTION

"I don't feel like I choose to cut—I feel like cutting chooses me. Most of the time it's like I'm a spectator rather than a participant. When it's done I look at my legs and go...what was that?"

Kara, age 19

Self-injury has only recently been the subject of serious study and research. There's still much to be learned about what makes this behavior so difficult to stop. But in recent years the notion of self-injury as addiction has become commonplace in the literature.

There are some who are uncomfortable calling a behavioral pattern an *addiction*, because the term is most commonly applied to the abuse of substances. These individuals might prefer to call the repetitive return to a particular behavior a *compulsion*. But whether we refer to self-injury as an addiction or a compulsion isn't really the point. Either concept is rooted in the understanding that what is happening no longer feels like a choice.

People who are honest enough to admit they are addicted to food, drugs, or alcohol will tell you their eating, snorting, smoking, or drinking has reached the point where they've lost their ability to choose not to do it. The same is true for many who self-injure. I can't count the number of times I've heard a cutter say, "I just can't not do it. I tell myself over and over that I won't do it again—and then...I do it again."

AM I TALKING TO YOU?

A lot of kids who self-injure believe they can quit hurting themselves anytime they want to. Unfortunately, it's usually not that simple. As you read this next chapter, I want you to ask yourself honestly where you are in this cycle of addiction you're going to learn about. The first step in breaking any addiction is admitting that you've become powerless to stop what it is you're doing. If that's where you're at, I beg you to be honest enough to admit you need help.

Whatever the Cost

When experts describe the dynamics of a true addiction, one key factor is that the addictive substance or behavior is pursued relentlessly, without any regard for the significant personal, physical, relational, spiritual, or emotional pain it will cause. The addict seems unable to calculate the huge imbalance between the short-term pleasure a particular substance might produce and the long-term loss he or she will be left with once the buzz has worn off. The consequences are simply not a factor. Before long, the loss of personal volition makes it feel like it's no longer a choice—it "just happens." In the same way, though the losses associated with self-injury are immense, they apparently are not enough to outweigh the anticipated momentary benefit.

Virtually every addictive pattern begins as a pursuit of pleasure. Alcohol has the potential to induce a sense of relaxation and calm. Troubles disappear. Anxiety wanes. The TV commercials with beautiful people in designer clothes sharing drinks in a perfect setting promise that alcohol will fill our deepest longings for connection and community. What a contrast with the reality of alcoholics who lose their ability to choose. In a very real sense repetitive self-injury does the very same thing. In its early stages it produces highly desirable effects—it can mask or control pain, cause one to be noticed and cared for, or provide a temporary sense of calm and control. But these highly desirable outcomes last only for shorter and shorter periods of time. Recently, Josh explained to me how disappointing his recent bruising and burning episodes had been for him:

> *I used to feel good for at least a couple of days after hurting myself. But now I'm lucky if it feels good for 10 minutes. I'm having to hit harder and do it more often just to keep going.*

Those of us who have not engaged in this kind of behavior may find it difficult to understand the positive affect that accompanies those first few episodes. But we can believe the reports of kids who know from personal experience. The impact is immediate and powerful. The illusion of being back in control is unmistakable. Unfortunately, the outcome is short-lived.

The Law of Diminishing Returns

There are some Scriptures that shed some significant light on this phenomenon. Proverbs 14:12 tells us, "There is a way that appears to be right, but in the end it leads to death." Our foolish minds can lead us to believe we've found a solution—a path to life—and our first few steps on that path may affirm that we're on the right track. Only when it's too late do we discover that our chosen path leads to a disastrous end.

The prophet Jeremiah offers some additional insights to help us understand how this works in real life. In Jeremiah 2:13, he speaks the word of the Lord to his fellow Israelites: "My people have committed two sins: They have forsaken me, the spring of living water, and have dug their own cisterns, broken cisterns that cannot hold water." A cistern was a device used to gather rainwater on the rare occasions when it would fall. Jeremiah declares that God's people are ignoring a source of satisfaction that is refreshing and unending—a fountain that flows freely for all. That's sin number one. And here's the second: Instead of enjoying the free gift offered to them, they've tried to quench their thirst by stubbornly taking things into their own hands.

What makes a cistern attractive is that it's mine! It allows me to stay independent and manage my own needs on my own terms. But the problem is that it can't hold water. Do you see how this speaks to the kind of behavior we're talking about in this book? In a desperate attempt to feel safe and calm, to invite the involvement of people who matter, or to create safe distance from people who might cause pain, kids quite literally take things into their own hands. They sincerely believe they've found a solution to their deep problems, and it works in the short term. But in the end it leads to destruction.

The Path to Addiction

Let's take a closer look at the way a behavior like cutting can become an addiction. Imagine a horizontal line that separates positive emotions from negative ones. Above the line we find all the good feelings—such as joy, contentment, happiness, satisfaction, peacefulness, safety, control, well-being, and hope. Below the line, life is painful—full of emotions like depression, anxiety, sadness, despair, fear, anger, sorrow, loss, loneliness, and hopelessness.

Most kids will tell you their lives are a mixture of pleasant and unpleasant events, with relationships that generate both positive and negative emotions. That's how life is meant to be and as people mature emotionally and spiritually they learn to live with that mix. But the experience of kids who cut is often different from that norm. Many people who engage in self-injury (and other addictive behaviors like eating disorders or substance abuse) tell stories of lives mostly lived "below the line." The painful feelings that mark their days are often the result of abandonment, neglect, abuse, and betrayal. Life is tough for these kids. In the already chaotic emotional world of adolescence, these feelings of hopelessness and despair demand relief. The kids feel as if their lives are spiraling out of control.

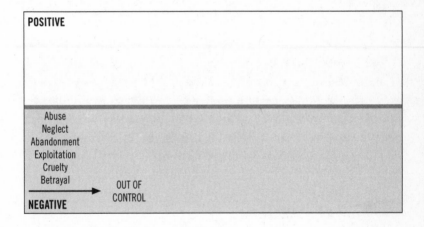

It's at this point, in a desperate attempt to change how they are feeling, that some kids stumble onto the idea of hurting themselves. The reason self-injury seems like a reasonable solution varies from story to story—perhaps it's something they've heard about at school or through the media, or maybe—as we're seeing more and more often—they try it at the suggestion of someone else who's already self-injuring. Whatever it is that motivates the first experience, some kids find that hurting themselves lifts them out of despair instantly and gives them the sense they are back in control again.

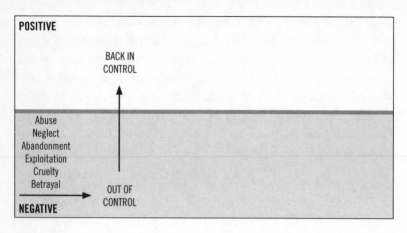

Of course, the relief from feelings of anxiety, hopelessness, or anger lasts only a short time. When that brief reprieve is over, they are plunged back into their world of hurt and pain again. But this time their negative feelings may be even more intense because there is the added burden of guilt, embarrassment, shame, and fear about what they've done.

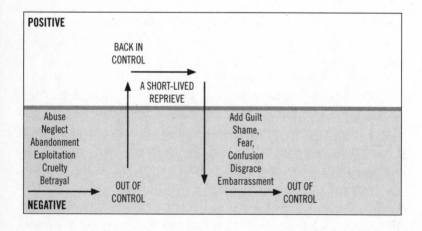

But the great news—as far as they're concerned—is that they now know how to "solve" these feelings. It's not socially acceptable, there's some physical pain involved... they all know that. But those familiar feelings of being emotionally chaotic and out of control lead them back to the solution that worked the last time. And so the cycle begins.

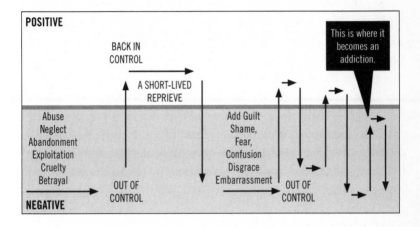

Unfortunately, the reprieve kids get from the self-injurious behavior quickly becomes susceptible to what's known as the "law of diminishing returns." What worked yesterday doesn't work as well today. That little cut doesn't do it anymore—or if it does, the good feelings don't last as long as they once did. In fact, as with other addictive behaviors, at some point the pleasure that was present in the beginning is no longer even a factor. *At some point it's just about not hurting so much anymore.*

This is critical to understand! When the behavior is no longer able to lift a kid's emotions above the line into "positive territory," it's no longer about feeling in control or gaining this sense of peacefulness that some cutters report. It's about not having to hurt anymore. Now the behavior is driven only by a subconscious need to be out of pain rather than by its ability to produce pleasure. In most cases the sense of consciously "choosing" the behavior is lost. That's when a behavior becomes truly addictive—it no longer feels like a choice.

It's at this point a self-injurer confronts the same dilemma the person on the brink of any addiction faces. The "cistern" has run dry and no longer gives any satisfaction to their thirsty souls. This leaves these deeply hurting kids with very few choices. Some move on to other short-term solutions, which in turn create the same dissatisfaction and disappointment. (This may be why we see so many cutters who also abuse alcohol and other drugs, engage in destructive sexual activity, have eating disorders, or participate in a variety of other dead-end behaviors.)

Other self-injurers find they can make it work again by intensifying the experience somehow. In some cases that means cutting more often. Perhaps the monthly ritual turns weekly. For others it means cutting more aggressively. Here's how Heather describes it:

> The neat thin razor lines just weren't doing it for me anymore. I was making a sandwich one day at lunch and as I was cutting a slice from a fresh loaf of bread my mom had baked I saw that rough serrated edge of the bread knife hacking its way through. I had just discovered my new best friend.

I've watched kids move from one or two shallow razor cuts to frantic sessions where a dozen or more deep wounds are inflicted. Sometimes the transition takes place over the course of just a few weeks or months. I've seen others shift from simple cuts to carved words expressing self-contempt or deep woundedness. Kids who start by burning themselves with matches or cigarette butts move on to experiment with scalding water or caustic acids. The sad reality is that no form of self-harm—no matter how frequent, no matter how aggressive, no matter how permanent—is able to accomplish what the self-injurer desperately hopes it will. Cutting, burning, or bruising may feel like a friend to some kids, but it's a lying friend—promising what it cannot deliver and then leaving deeply hurting kids with permanent reminders of their shame and brokenness.

There's one more insight related to the addictive nature of self-harm that should be mentioned, although research in this area is just beginning to emerge. We've talked about how self-injury can actually produce a physiologically positive effect in the body. It may very well be that the chemicals generated in response to the body's pain could be addictive in the same way other chemical substances are. Current research being done in this area may help us better understand the relentless grip self-injury has on those who trust it to solve their problems.

DON'T TRY TO MAKE ME! WHY THEY CAN'T/WON'T STOP

"I've quit cutting about a thousand times—once for over a month but mostly just for a week or so. I know it's a stupid dead end and it's easy to decide never to do it again—until I'm alone in my room after a crappy day at school and I feel gross and I just had a fight with my mom and grabbing the knife seems like the most logical thing in the world."

Lisa, age 16

Shannon sat in my office, carefully folding, unfolding, and refolding the tissue that was keeping her hands busy. We'd met a half-dozen times to talk about the cutting, burning, and hair-pulling that had become a regular part of her life about three years earlier. What had started as an occasional way to release stress during exams, before basketball tournaments, or when things got particularly ugly at home had gradually become a more and more frequent occurrence. She told me her cutting was no longer necessarily related to a particularly stressful incident. "In fact," she told me, "some days it feels like just not cutting is what gives me stress."

Shannon recognized that a strategy that once gave her a feeling of control had now taken control of her life. "I've got to stop," she declared, clenching the tissue in her fist. "I can't keep living like this—it's insane. I'm telling you right now—that's it! I've cut for the last time. I'm never doing it again."

As I listened to her, I experienced the same conflicting emotions I've felt when other self-injurers I've known get to the place of deciding it's time to quit. On one hand I feel a genuine sense of joy in knowing they are preparing to turn an important corner. It's impossible for me to drag them around that corner without their desire and participation. Deciding they've had enough and verbally expressing that to another person is an important first step.

But I have to admit that my joy in knowing they're ready to move ahead is accompanied by a fear that comes from having been at this place with lots of kids before. And I know that, in spite of their good intentions, there are some huge hurdles still to be cleared. Old patterns of thinking need to be challenged and new patterns need to be developed. Transformation can come about only as a result of a renewed mind (Romans 12:2). Challenging the old patterns and assumptions that lead to self-injuring is tougher than most people realize.

It's Just Not That Easy

Most acts of self-injury are based on twisted thinking. As we've discovered earlier, the behavior is often motivated by inaccurate but unchallenged assumptions that kids make about themselves based on their interpretation of life's events and relationships. These interpretations lead to patterns of behavior that feel non-volitional (like they're not a conscious choice). As these patterns progress, they develop an ever stronger grip. Even when a self-injurer sincerely desires freedom, he or she may find that cycles of irrational thought make it extremely difficult to act on this desire.

For those of us who love and care for self-injurers, confronting these stubborn patterns of thinking can be frustrating and draining. From the outside looking in, self-injury makes no sense at all. In the mind of anyone who's thinking clearly, it might seem as if it should be relatively easy to stop. Unfortunately, most self-injurers aren't thinking clearly. Even after having made a decision to stop, they find themselves rationalizing their behaviors with arguments that seem to justify "just one more" episode.

The dilemma is familiar to anyone who's ever been trapped in an addiction. The alcoholic can always come up with a reason for just one more drink. The overeater decides to supersize just one more meal. The anorexic persuades herself that losing another couple of pounds is perfectly reasonable. The pornography addict clicks his way to just one more look.

Confronting the Lies with Truth

In the work I've done with kids who self-injure, I've found there are a number of typical arguments routinely offered as reasons for continuing the behavior or as means for minimizing the guilt associated with "just one more time." In order to help kids follow through on their commitment to stop self-destructive behavior, it will be necessary for you to be aware of these lies and prepared to help by confronting them with truth. Each of the following lies represents distorted thinking that must be replaced by healthy, renewed thinking.

Lie 1: "My choice to self-injure doesn't affect anyone but me."

When kids spend their whole lives feeling like failures, they may conclude they are disappointments to everyone around them. Often kids like this feel responsible whenever things go wrong in their family, on their team, or in their circle of friends.

They live with the guilt of believing it's always their fault. They become cautious, sometimes to a point of paranoia, about interacting with people around them. The fear of blowing it and ruining it for someone else inhibits their every move.

These kids often withdraw to the point where they share their lives with no one. In all likelihood, their past attempts to share their feelings led to rejection rather than acceptance. "Why are you always so angry?" "You bring the whole family down with your depression." "Your dad and I have been really worried about you lately. We've got enough stress in our lives as it is. Don't do this to us!" Words like these communicate a clear message to kids that their problems are a bother to everyone around. These kids believe they need to find a way to suck it up and deal with their issues in a way that doesn't ruin life for everyone else. For these kids, self-injury may seem like a reasonable alternative, because it appears to be one coping mechanism that doesn't directly impact the lives of anyone else. And in the short term they may be right—if no one's noticing, it's possible that no one is affected, at first.

A POINT FOR PARENTS

There are times when, due to our own deep hurt, fear, and confusion, we may communicate to our kids that their choices are making us into victims. "After all I've done for you I can't believe you would do this to me." As cathartic as that might feel to say some days, it usually destroys rather than builds relationship. It turns into a no-win "you're hurting me more than I hurt you" conversation that can't produce positive results.

Of course, the truth is that many people are affected by someone's choice to self-injure. It creates disruption in families and fear in friends. One person's decision to deal with his or her pain in this unhealthy way could give permission to others to do the same, starting them on their own path to destruction.

There's evidence that cutting behaviors can be highly "contagious." A study done of teenagers in a group home in Canada found that when a self-injurer was admitted to a home where no one had been self-injuring, it was only a short time until several others had taken up the habit.

And then there's the effect a self-injurer's choices will have on his or her future relationships. As we discussed earlier in the book, there are huge implications for spouses, friends, and even children who may one day need to have "mommy's sore arms" explained to them. Our choices do impact others.

In fact, at one level, self-injury could be viewed as a very selfish act. It does not take into account the feelings of others either in the present or the future. For the kid who cuts, it provides the outcome desired in that moment with little or no regard for how it impacts others. The lie that self-injury affects no one else is challenged by the truth of these words from Paul in 1 Corinthians 12:25-26.

> "There should be no division in the body, but that its parts should have equal concern for each other. If one part suffers, every part suffers with it; if one part is honored, every part rejoices with it."

Lie 2: "This is my body and I can do whatever I want with it."

Too many kids have had their bodies abused or taken advantage of in some inappropriate way. We've already discussed the strong correlation between sexual abuse and self-injury. To be sexually abused is to lose the sense of control over one's own body. Some types of abuse are violent and overpowering, while others are more seductive and manipulative, but in either case the victim is left feeling powerless and vulnerable. There is an immediate and urgent need to regain some sense of ownership. For most victims of abuse, the dream of ever feeling comfortable in one's own skin or feeling good about one's body seems unreachable. They may find themselves simply wanting to reclaim whatever ownership they can. Self-injurers declare to themselves—and perhaps to anyone else who notices—that they have taken back their own bodies. To declare, "This is mine!" provides at least an illusion of power and safety.

Don't assume, however, that an overt act of sexual assault or abuse is a necessary prerequisite for feelings of vulnerability. In our highly sexualized culture, both guys and girls may feel an inordinate amount of uneasiness around their sexuality. On most high school campuses bodies are scrutinized, compared, ogled, and discussed at length. Kids feel incredible pressure to offer their bodies to one another even in casual friendships. It's not surprising that some of them end up feeling their bodies aren't their own.

A HINT FOR HELPERS

The kind of listening, discerning, and responding required in working with kids who cut is often far beyond what any of us can do in our own strength and wisdom. If we are to be Jesus to these kids, we will need to understand the power of prayer and the value of being spiritually tuned in to the still small voice of God. We should never try to be Jesus on our own power alone. Remember we don't have to do it on our own—he has promised to give us his power and presence (Matthew 28:18-20).

But here's the truth. There is a very real sense in which our bodies are indeed our own. They are a gift our loving Creator offers to each of us that we might enjoy life to the fullest. Psalm 139:14 reminds us that we are "fearfully and wonderfully made." Having acknowledged that our bodies are our own, we must recognize that this does not give us license to use them in any way we please. In fact we are urged in Romans 12:1 to offer our bodies as "a living sacrifice." God's desire is for us to enjoy our physical bodies and to take responsibility for creating appropriate boundaries to ensure we use them in ways that honor him.

In 1 Corinthians 6:19-20 we see a statement of truth that challenges the lie that says, "It's my body, so I can do whatever I want with it." Paul is speaking in this passage about making wise sexual choices, but I believe the principle applies much more broadly.

> "Do you not know that your bodies are temples of the Holy Spirit, who is in you, whom you have received from God? You are not your own; you were bought at a price. Therefore honor God with your bodies."

Lie 3: "If I stop cutting, I won't have any effective way of dealing with my pain."

Most kids who choose self-harm as a way of dealing with their pain have already attempted a variety of other strategies. Perhaps they tried to talk to someone about the hurt they were feeling. Perhaps they filled journals with their thoughts or expressed their emotions through art or music. Some may have thrown themselves intensely into their academic studies or tried to find affirmation by succeeding in athletics. It's not unusual for kids who self-injure to have dabbled in drugs, abused alcohol, become involved in inappropriate sexual behavior, or used food in unhealthy ways to try to reduce their hurt. We already know what they found out—the best these strategies offer is a temporary fix.

Many kids who attempt self-injury find that it really works at first—maybe better than anything else they've tried. So when they consider giving up such behavior, their practical concern is that they'll be left only with options that have already proved to be ineffective.

This is a difficult lie to challenge. The pain is real and it demands relief. Right now, they've found a solution that's working. Yes, the price is high, but the payoff is immediate and the cutter feels very much in control.

At this point our role is not to suggest an alternative; our role is to be the alternative. We know ultimate healing will come only when the deep wounds can be touched by the healing hands of Jesus. But for now we are his hands, his ears, and his voice. With his Spirit in us, we can listen deeply, speak hope into despair, and deliver healing we would be incapable of offering on our own.

This means we choose to offer relationship to kids who are cautious and remain distant because their trust has been betrayed in the past. This means we provide community for kids who may have never felt like they belong. This means we speak words of hope even before kids are prepared to embrace the truth. In all of this we point them to the One who will bring true healing to the deepest places in their hearts.

Peter understands what it means to direct people to that place of hope. The truth of 1 Peter 5:7 is as firm today as it ever was, and it calls kids away from the lie that self-injuring is the only answer to their problems.

> *"Cast all your anxiety on him because he cares for you."*

Lie 4: "If I don't self-injure, people won't know how much I hurt inside."

Often kids who have experienced abandonment or neglect develop the feeling that no one really takes them seriously—no one believes what they say or understands how they feel. Their lives are marked by a lonely longing for someone who will pay attention. Through observation or personal experience, they've learned that one way to get involvement from people around them is to be needy, weak, and hurt—and not just a little bit hurt but very hurt. Although they know the hurt inside them is intense and real, it's invisible—and they feel the need to validate it by finding a way to demonstrate or express it externally. They're afraid that if they just *tell* someone they are sad, afraid, angry, or lonely, they'll be told they're making a big deal out of nothing—that they just need to get over it, put on a happy face, and move on. But an actual physical wound is a whole different deal. When the evidence is visible, no one can deny its reality or its seriousness.

These kids fear that if they give up self-injury they'll have no way to invite anyone into their lives. Their scars have become so much a part of their identity that they don't even know who they'd be without them. On some subconscious level, they may believe that, without their visible wounds to demonstrate how deeply in crisis they are, they'll disappear and cease to exist at all.

The challenge of responding to this lie is that those kids who believe it do so because they've experienced the loneliness of life without wounds. So how do we respond to the teenagers who literally demand involvement by being so aggressively needy that they cannot be ignored?

The secret is to develop the kind of quality relationship with these kids that allows us to speak very frankly about how we experience them. This means building a deep level of mutual trust and respect—the key word is *mutual*—that will give us a platform from which we can speak truth in love. We will need to affirm their desire for relationship, but challenge the means by which they seek to obtain it.

It's not inappropriate to let kids know that when they attempt to manipulate us into spending time and energy with them, it can actually make us less motivated to do so. We can affirm our commitment to them by showing we enjoy time with them without their having to create a crisis. Once the issue has been raised, we can take opportunities to lovingly but firmly point out examples of emotionally manipulative behaviors as they occur: "This is what we were talking about the other day. When you kick into that helpless, demanding mode it actually makes me want to walk away rather than walking toward you. But I'd love to hear about what's going on in your life right now—why don't you just ask if you can talk to me?"

Christian community should be a place of refuge for those who are hurting. But in order to function that way, we must be highly committed to acting lovingly toward one another. In response to the lie that no one will notice their pain unless they cut, we must offer hurting kids the truth of a community that is sensitive to their needs and seeks to build them up. Ephesians 4:29 reminds us that such community expresses itself in healthy communication:

> "Do not let any unwholesome talk come out of your mouths, but only what is helpful for building others up according to their needs, that it may benefit those who listen."

Lie 5: "I need to cut, so people won't get close enough that they can hurt me."

Kids who cut have often experienced the betrayal of the people closest to them. In some cases these people include parents, grandparents, siblings, and others who should be thoroughly trustworthy. More routinely, the betrayal comes from friends who fail to follow through on promises or blatantly reject them right when support is most needed.

Those of us who work in youth ministry can inadvertently become part of this cycle of betrayal. Maybe it's the small group leader who quits just when his guys were starting to trust him. Or the youth pastor who moves to a new church, leaving behind a youth group that has to get to know a new leader (probably after a year of having no one at all). Or the coach who cuts the kid from the team. These situations can be deep disappointments for kids, and they may feel betrayed by the adult responsible. This can create a fear and mistrust that makes such kids feel as if they never want to get close to anyone again.

AM I TALKING TO YOU?

You know how deeply you long for someone to be there for you. You need to start reconnecting with people around you. My guess is that you are probably pushing away the people who love you the most. Of course, letting them back means you risk being hurt again, but I invite you to begin risking again. You were created for connection. Go slowly at first, but don't allow yourself to stay locked in the lonely world you've created.

Self-injurers know that the sight of scars or fresh wounds will keep most people away. Even those who never see the actual evidence may hear rumors and keep their distance. Although the cutter longs for relationship, the fear of intimacy trumps that desire. Kids may find a sense of power in knowing they can keep people at bay simply by perpetuating their reputation for engaging in a bizarre behavior no one seems to understand.

At the heart of this lie is the belief that intimacy automatically equals hurt and disappointment. The majority of these kids have never had relationships that challenge this belief. Most of their significant relationships have reinforced the notion that whenever they allow themselves to need someone, they end up being hurt.

Behind the tough façade these kids use to push people away, we know our Creator has placed within each of them a genuine desire to belong and to be loved. These kids need to taste true Christian community and to experience relationships with people they can count on. It would be especially meaningful for them to be in relationship with caring adults who are committed to seeing them through the ups and downs inherent in the coping strategies they've chosen.

The only way this lie that seeks to keep people away can be meaningfully challenged is relationally. Talking about it won't make any difference. Preaching won't convince them. The kids have to experience what it is to be cared for by someone who genuinely loves them.

The problem with offering these kids the love they need is that their first response will be to reject it. It takes someone with substantial resilience to endure the slings and arrows sure to be fired in your direction if you try to build a relationship with a kid who is committed to resisting intimacy. But it's not optional.

In my experience, breaking the cycle of self-injury always involves the element of loving community and trustworthy relationship. In order to shatter the lie that says the cutter can find safety only by keeping others away, we must love one another. For Jesus told his disciples in John 13:34-35 that the truth of the gospel is validated by the kind of relationships we offer one another:

> *"A new command I give you: Love one another. As I have loved you, so you must love one another. By this everyone will know that you are my disciples, if you love one another."*

Lie 6: "I'm still guilty, and I could never punish myself enough."

The Bible tells us Satan is an accuser (Revelation 12:10). The implication is that he finds great delight in pointing his bony finger to remind people of their faults and failures. Kids who give in to the lure of self-injury are often particularly vulnerable to guilt trips. They live with unchallenged assumptions that remind them constantly that they are failures. If their self-injury has been motivated by the conviction that they need to be punished, they may have a deep belief that they can never be fully forgiven.

We discussed earlier the way in which each of our lives represents a mixture of victimization and agency. This means that, even though many kids we work with have horrendous tales of pain caused by others, there are probably areas of their lives where they also need to experience forgiveness. One big challenge is in helping them sort through the real guilt from that which has been illegitimately self-inflicted. I've often found these adolescents are inclined to punish themselves for who they are rather than for what they've done. When I see the words *ugly, stupid,* and *unlovable* carved on a girl's arm and she tells me she's cutting because she is those things, I recognize she's confused her need for forgiveness (which will bring freedom from guilt) with her need for acceptance (which will bring genuine hope and healing.)

The good news of the gospel is that it addresses both needs. In the face of the lie that tells a self-injuring teen she is neither acceptable nor forgivable, the truth she must hear and embrace is that she is fully accepted and fully forgiven. It's a story of grace and mercy. Grace means we are loved lavishly without ever having to do anything to earn it. Mercy means we are forgiven and freed from the consequences of our choices. Paul talks enthusiastically about this truth in Colossians 1:13-14:

> *"For he has rescued us from the dominion of darkness and brought us into the kingdom of the Son he loves, in whom we have redemption, the forgiveness of sins."*

Lie 7: "If I give up self-injury, I'll end up doing something even worse."

Like a number of the others, this lie is rooted in fear. Most self-injurers realize their actions are an extreme response to the pain they feel. They've already eliminated a whole range of less intense strategies for managing their emotions. They realize that if they give this up they don't have a lot of options left.

The specific fear of many self-injurers, of course, is that the decision to stop harming themselves could ultimately lead to suicide. This gives us some sense of how close to the edge many of these kids find themselves living. In a very real sense self-injury is what's keeping them alive. This underscores how important it is for us to recognize that these kids view their behavior as self-care rather than self-mutilation or self-abuse.

When confronting this lie it's essential to intentionally affirm the young person's desire to stay alive. Self-injurers pay a huge price to ensure that suicide does not become an option. Their perseverance and resilience is something worthy of celebration. We must recognize their strong survival instinct and remind them of how important this strength will be as they explore other, less destructive strategies for staying alive.

AM I TALKING TO YOU?

If you feel yourself slipping toward feelings of such despair that you don't want to stay alive anymore, please tell someone—a trusted friend, a teacher or coach at school, a pastor or counselor—or even call a suicide hotline. You've obviously worked so hard to stay alive! As Good Charlotte said so well: "Hold on when you feel like letting go." If you've been coping by hurting yourself, some people will assume you've found a way to make it work. But if it's not working anymore, you'll need to invite someone else to help you.

We can assure self-injurers that their desire to stay alive is perfectly mirrored by Jesus' desire to give them true life. He promises in John 10:10 that his desire to give us life is the exact opposite of what the Enemy is hoping for. In response to the lie that tells them that their only path away from self-injury is death itself, we can promise the abundance, life, and passion we are meant to experience in relationship with the One whose name is Truth:

> *"The thief comes only to steal and kill and destroy; I have come that they may have life, and have it to the full."*

In an earlier chapter I suggested that spiritual warfare is a significant driving force behind the destructiveness of self-injury. The lies we've just explored illustrate perfectly the nature of that warfare. Satan twists and distorts the truth, clothing his lies attractively and luring people to believe he is trustworthy. It should be apparent we can respond effectively to these life-destroying lies only with the truth of God's Word—the truth embodied in Christ, who is "the way and the truth and the life" (John 14:6).

HELPING SELF- INJURERS FIND HOPE AND HEALING

"All praise to the God and Father of our Master, Jesus the Messiah! Father of all mercy! God of all healing counsel! He comes alongside us when we go through hard times, and before you know it, he brings us alongside someone else who is going through hard times so that we can be there for that person just as God was there for us."

2 Corinthians 1:3-4, *The Message*

Given everything we've learned about this world of hurt, how do we respond? I often feel overwhelmed as I think about finding ways to help kids who are struggling with self-injury and all that leads to it. The issues seem so immense, the destructive behaviors so deeply entrenched, and the pat answers that flood my mind so irrelevant. But we are called to "carry each other's burdens" (Galatians 6:2). Refusing to get involved is simply not an option.

The good news is that what we have to offer really matters. If you learn that someone you care about has been self-injuring, you have an opportunity to provide the loving support that can make a huge difference. If a young person trusts you enough to have shared the deepest secrets of his or her story with you, that's amazingly significant. It's unusual for adolescents to have that kind of faith in people—especially those who are older than they are. If a hurting young person has chosen to share with you at this level, it's safe to assume that he or she must believe you have something to offer.

When we learn that a teenager we love is involved in self-harming behavior, the biggest mistake we could possibly make is to walk away. There are plenty of reasons we might be tempted to do just that—the uncertainty that comes with not knowing what to do; the fear of doing the wrong thing and making the situation worse; the realization that this will take a massive amount of time and energy; and the knowledge that working with deeply hurting kids may stir up unresolved issues from our own adolescence. I'm guessing you could add a few reasons of your own.

One of the biggest reasons you might want to walk away is because you don't have any idea how you can fix the problem. So let me share another bit of good news, which might not sound so good at first: You can't fix anybody. If there's anything I've learned in my years of spending time with kids who cut, it's that God is the One who accomplishes the healing in their lives. He is the One who can transform death to life, despair to hope, brokenness to wholeness, and sadness to joy.

But for reasons I don't fully understand, God allows mere mortals like us to participate in the miraculous work he is able to do in the lives of the students who invite us into their stories. It is God who gives us discernment to listen wisely. It is God who gives us words to respond appropriately. It is God who gives us energy to carry on when we feel we have nothing more to offer.

And it is God who continues to bring about change in our own lives as we submit ourselves to his purposes and make ourselves available to kids who need us.

First Things First

It probably goes without saying that kids who are involved in habitual, repetitive self-injury will likely need professional help. When physical violence toward oneself seems like a reasonable response to life's stresses, the situation is pretty serious. Do everything you can to help these families or individuals find the kind of professional support they need. It might be difficult to find a therapist trained in dealing with this particular disorder, but don't lose heart. Remember that self-injury represents the tip of an iceberg—beneath the surface are all sorts of relational, emotional, and spiritual issues that a good counselor can help deal with effectively.

A HINT FOR HELPERS

Make sure you are aware of the professionals in your community who could be helpful in dealing with these tough issues. Create a little phone list of names and numbers of medical doctors, therapists, toll-free hotlines, school counselors, and parenting coaches to whom you can refer people. Talk to other folks dealing with this issue who might be able to recommend additional resource persons. And, as I said at the beginning of the book, if you are anticipating a life as a mental-health professional, I'd urge you to consider the possibility of specializing in dealing with adolescents at risk. It's difficult work, but I'll guarantee job security!

But don't assume your job is done once you've referred your self-harming friend to a therapist. A professional counselor can offer certain kinds of support that you're probably not equipped to provide. But you are able to offer the kind of ongoing relationship that most therapists can't possibly give all their clients. Your role as a friend, encourager, listener, accountability partner, and even first-aid consultant is crucial to the overall healing journey. Both relationships are necessary for a positive outcome.

Becoming the Kind of Person Who Can Help

So how do we help bring hope and healing to kids who cut? If God has brought us alongside someone who's going through hard times, how can we be there for that hurting kid in the way Paul suggests in the Scripture that opens this chapter?

It will begin by becoming the kind of person who truly can help. Your most significant instrument of ministry is your life, lived visibly so the kids you come in contact with will see the difference the gospel makes in you. There are a number of qualities that seem to be consistently present in people who prove to be effective in helping kids who self-harm. You'll notice that many of these qualities mirror the character of Jesus—not surprising, since our role is to represent him in the lives of these kids. Follow along as I attempt to paint a portrait of an effective helper.

- *Humility:* If we want to be effective helpers, we must begin by recognizing our own limitations. Are we willing to ask for help when we find ourselves in over our heads? We are privileged to participate with Jesus in bringing hope to hurting kids, but we must remember he is the "Wonderful Counselor" (Isaiah 9:6). As humble helpers we must understand the value of prayer and consciously acknowledge our dependence on God. Working with kids who self-harm can be a thankless job. There's very little applause and the going is slow. People who need instant gratification or lots of visible evidence of success won't last long.

- *Authenticity:* Most hurting kids are desperate to find an adult who is comfortable enough to be completely authentic. Authenticity simply means that what you see is what you get. Teenagers have a finely tuned "hypocrisy detector" that instantly sniffs out posers and wannabes. They are looking for an adult who will truly love them—even if they don't fit neatly into the box. They are looking for someone who's willing to be honest about their own questions and struggles, instead of offering up clichés and pat answers. They are looking for someone who's emotionally alive and willing to feel the pain behind the story. Authenticity means weeping with those who weep and rejoicing with those who rejoice (Romans 12:15). It's essentially about letting kids know we are trustworthy. If they don't sense authenticity, there will be no trust; if there is no trust, there will be no relationship; and if there's no relationship, there will be no opportunity for influence.

• *Acceptance:* Kids who cut expect to be rejected by those with whom they long to be in relationship. They're used to being abandoned and neglected. The fact that their bodies are scarred and their hearts are broken makes them feel even more unacceptable. In response to the powerful shame they feel, self-injurers may engage in other behaviors socially unacceptable and, frankly, obnoxious at times. They'll do things that might drive other people away just to test if our acceptance is authentic. There are days when it takes an extra measure of grace to love these kids in a way that communicates that they are acceptable. As we seek to do so, let's never forget that this is exactly what Jesus did for us.

• *Gentleness:* In spite of the tough exterior many self-injuring kids hide behind, most of them are fragile and vulnerable inside. Just as physical wounds that are healing need to be treated with tenderness, so too must soul wounds be protected from further harm. We must recognize that our thoughtless words or careless actions could potentially do further damage to a hurting kid. Gentleness communicates to kids that they are safe with us. Pray that Psalm 141:3 will be true: "Set a guard over my mouth, LORD; keep watch over the door of my lips." Gentle helpers are kind and nurturing, willing to create a protected space where kids feel safe enough to be honest as they take their first shaky steps toward wholeness.

• *Firmness:* When it comes to helping kids who self-injure, only the strong survive. Those who last for the long haul do so out of an inner strength not easily shaken. The stories we hear are heart wrenching, the wounds we are asked to assess are real, and the decisions we sometimes must make are tough. The firmness I'm talking about here stands in contrast to mere strength or power because it is always tempered by the gentleness discussed in the previous point. Firmness means we are not easily sucked in by kids who are master manipulators. Firmness means we maintain appropriate boundaries to protect our own marriages, families, and spiritual lives. Once self-injuring kids decide we are trustworthy, they will take absolutely everything we are willing to give them. With their needs looming so large, we can easily become imbalanced and unhealthy if we make ourselves too available. Most kids will respect a firm commitment to our boundaries, if these boundaries are communicated in a spirit of love and care.

• *Willingness To Be Well Informed:* Although there's still much that's unknown about the dynamics of self-injury, there is a growing body of literature that gives us significant insight into this specialized field of study. If we hope to be effective in the work we do with kids who cut, it is essential to be as well informed as we can be. At the end of the book, you will find appendixes that list a number of books, Web sites, and organizations that will help you stay aware of the latest research. Keep an eye out for training events that may be happening in your area and TV documentaries that deal with the topic. Above all, learn everything you can from the kids you talk with—both those who self-injure and those who know other kids who do. There are some things you can only learn by encountering them firsthand.

• *Hopefulness:* One of the defining characteristics of kids who self-injure is despair. They feel trapped in a cycle that feels like it has no end. When they feel without hope, we have the opportunity to be hopeful for them. Such hope is not based on our own optimism that we can be of help. Nor is it based in our faith that they will tenaciously follow through on the process they've begun. Our hope is in the God who promises to make all things new (2 Corinthians 5:17). It is his faithfulness in our own lives that gives us the courage to invite kids to a similar journey. The path toward healing and wholeness will require a great deal of these kids—in fact, it will require their all. Do we understand that level of commitment in our own spiritual journeys? It would be unethical to encourage a young person to take risks we have not been willing to take.

But It's Not *Just* about Who You Are

While it's important to develop the qualities that will make us the kinds of people who can help, we can't stop there. It's equally essential to learn the skills necessary to respond appropriately to the underlying dynamics of the self-injurious cycle.

In this final section, we'll briefly review a few of the primary themes that pervade the thinking of most self-injurers, and then talk about how we can address each of them most effectively. As Romans 12:2 reminds us, the transformation in behavior we seek must begin with the renewing of the mind. But in our efforts to encourage self-injuring kids toward the renewed thinking, *the bottom line is that we must respond relationally.* Much of the damage that leads to self-harming behavior is rooted in broken or unhealthy relationships. Perhaps that's why it's important for us to deliver a message of hope and healing in the context of a healthy, nurturing relationship.

Self-Injuring Dynamic: Low Self-Esteem and a Sense of Personal Defectiveness

It's clear that kids who self-injure have an inappropriately negative view of themselves. As self-injurers compare themselves with their peers, they typically place themselves low on the social ladder. This has all sorts of practical implications that must be taken into account as we respond.

Relational Response: Affirm Character Qualities

When kids who cut look in the mirror, they don't tend to see much that's positive. Their deep disdain for their bodies diminishes the motivation to take care of themselves. You see it in their posture, you can't miss it in their facial expressions, and often even their wardrobes and personal hygiene will reflect their lack of care for themselves.

The relational antidote for low self-esteem is meaningful affirmation. What makes affirmation meaningful is when it focuses on things kids can actually take responsibility for. This means being intentional about looking for character qualities that can be affirmed rather than merely applauding performance or achievement. Qualities like persistence, patience, self-discipline, and generosity are what we want to encourage these kids to focus on. These are the qualities that will move them forward in their pursuit of healthy relationships. They need to be reminded often of the good things we see in them. Their lives have been filled with so many negative messages that the challenge of replacing them with legitimate positive messages will take our time and patience.

Relational Response: Provide Healthy Community

Typically, kids with low self-esteem will surround themselves with friends they believe to be in the same "league" as they are. As the old saying goes, "Birds of a feather flock together." This may mean the social circle of many self-injurers is made up of other equally unhealthy adolescents, who are often negative and unmotivated. It is imperative we help the kids we work with understand the value of friends who will lift them up rather than drag them down. Establishing communities of young people where kids can develop relationships with positive peers is a crucial part of this process.

To be honest I've found this to be one of the most difficult steps in the journey toward healing. The risks involved in giving up the familiar, safe friendships and risking rejection by opening oneself to others is something a lot of kids are reluctant to do. But I know very few kids who have been able to break the cycle of self-harm (or any other addictive behavior, for that matter) without making some major changes in their circle of friends. We must do all we can to provide opportunities for these kids to build new relationships that will help them grow.

Self-Injuring Dynamic: A Lifetime of Stuffed Emotions

Most self-injurers are emotionally unhealthy in one way or another. As we've discovered they are either driven by such intense emotions that they must find ways to cathartically vent them or they have so consistently denied their emotions that they find themselves feeling nothing at all.

Relational Response: Validate Emotions

Many cutters have been told in a variety of ways that what they feel doesn't really matter. They often conclude that what's going on inside them must be wrong. When negative emotions like sadness, fear, and anger are deemed inappropriate, it often leaves kids with no choice but to push those emotions to the back corners of their hearts.

Buried emotions fester in the soul, silently sapping life and robbing an individual of the freedom God seeks to provide. Self-injurers feel such a deep need to express these deeply held feelings that they are willing to damage their own bodies in a desperate attempt to let them out. By helping them understand that these emotions are appropriate and valid, by showing we are not afraid of their feelings nor will we reject them, we open a pathway to healing.

Relational Response: Listen Deeply

Listening is hard work. It requires we lay aside our personal agendas and give our full attention to the heart of another. Good listening is a skill that must be learned and practiced. There is nothing a self-injuring kid needs more than to talk freely, with someone that kid genuinely trusts, about the familiar emotions so much a part of his or her life. By being a good listener we offer kids an alternative to self-harm as a way of expressing and venting their stuffed emotions. Eventually we will have to help them learn appropriate ways to communicate their emotions and process their feelings, but the first stage is to simply listen. Here are a few suggestions to help you listen well:

- *Let them know you're willing to listen.* I've found that the best way to open a conversation is by saying something like, "I'd love to hear your story if you'd be willing to share it with me." As the story is being told, simple prompts like "tell me more about that day" or "what happened next?" let the storyteller know you are not tired of listening.

- *Keep your mouth shut.* Your natural tendency may be to jump in with quick advice and premature questions. Listening quietly is a discipline that must be developed. Evaluate one of your next conversations with a hurting kid by reflecting on the amount of time they talked in comparison with the amount of time *you* had the floor.

• *Be prepared for intensity.* When kids finally feel permission to express pent-up emotions, the combination of self-contempt, anger, fear, and deep sadness may come out with a great deal of energy. The language may be rough. In the e-mail I got last night from one of the kids I'm working with, I counted 24 uses of "the f-word" in its various forms (noun, verb, adjective, adverb, and even as a complete sentence a few times), and that was just the opening paragraph! I was happy he felt safe enough with me to share his anguish at that level. You'll need to get used to clenched fists, angry outbursts, and lots of tears. When kids are willing to share the true depth of their feelings with you, they are communicating that they genuinely trust you. Accept that as an honor.

• *Be comfortable with silence.* Make space for kids to reflect on what's going on inside as they tell their stories. In many cases they are encountering emotions they've denied themselves for a long time. It's as though they're going back to a place they haven't visited recently—especially if they're talking about emotions rather than merely events. Staying silent gives them time to process as they go.

• *Let your body show you're listening.* Things like eye contact, an engaged posture, and appropriate nods will let kids know you're tracking with them. Don't assume you're good at this. I've watched videotapes of sessions I was doing and was appalled at how often I fidgeted and appeared disengaged from the process.

• *Pray as you listen.* Our human ears and sinful hearts are not capable of hearing all that needs to be heard or feeling all that needs to be felt as kids share their stories with us. A spirit of prayerfulness as we listen acknowledges our dependence on God and actually opens our hearts to hearing what only he can reveal to us. Confronting the lies of the Enemy and challenging thought patterns that are personally and relationally destructive is spiritual warfare. We will need Christ's resources if we hope for victory.

For a more complete discussion on how to listen well, you might want to look at my earlier book, *Help, My Kids Are Hurting*, where this topic is addressed more thoroughly.

Self-Injuring Dynamic: Feelings of Profound Abandonment

Kids who cut are lonely. In many cases it was neglect and abandonment that began their journey from self-doubt into self-destructiveness. Now their secret and its associated scars reinforce these feelings of defectiveness and unworthiness. Their deep thirst for love and belonging simply serves to intensify their belief that they are alone. In the face of these feelings, some kids aggressively push everyone away, while others just quietly melt into the background. Either way, it's important for us to reach out to them and proactively build bridges of relationship.

Relational Response: Offer Your Presence

Perhaps the most significant gift we can offer self-harming kids is the same gift Christ freely offers to us—presence. Just before Jesus ascended into heaven, he spoke the familiar words we refer to as the Great Commission. I've sometimes wondered if we should rename it the Great Promise, because it closes with Jesus assuring all his disciples, both then and now, that we can always count on his presence. "And surely I am with you always, to the very end of the age."

One deeply moving name we find for God in the Hebrew of the Old Testament is *Jehovah-Shammah*. It means, "the God who is there." The ultimate expression of that desire to be present with us is expressed in John 1:14: "The Word became flesh and made his dwelling among us. We have seen his glory, the glory of the one and only [Son], who came from the Father, full of grace and truth." The theological term for God's becoming flesh in Jesus is the *incarnation*. When we offer self-injuring kids our presence in the name of Jesus, we fulfill the ministry to which he called us. Sometimes we call this relational approach to youth ministry committed to being present with kids "incarnational youth ministry," because it expresses itself in intentionally entering a kid's world so the glory of the "one and only Son who came from the Father" will be seen again.

How many times have you heard teenagers say, "I don't feel like I have anyone who's *there* for me"? Their parents are too busy (many parents are much more comfortable offering their kids presents rather than presence). They can't count on their friends. Even if they pray, they may feel as if God's not listening. Into this emptiness we have the opportunity to come as Christ's representative.

Being "present" with hurting kids will require more from us than being in the same room. It means gently initiating relationship with kids who are relationally cautious because of past hurts. It means offering undivided attention when such attention is needed. It means being emotionally engaged with what's being shared. It means caring enough to be deeply impacted by the life of another. It means being available (with appropriate boundaries as we discussed earlier) so kids will know we have time for them.

Realistically, we can't offer our presence to an unlimited number of kids. This can be frustrating when our communities are full of kids with all kinds of needs. Ask God for the wisdom to determine which students you'll go deep with. Trust him to look after those whom you simply do not have time and energy to pursue, recognizing that as their good Father, he will find ways to minister to them.

Self-Injuring Dynamic: Feeling Trapped, Hopeless, or Despairing

Most kids who cut can see no way out of their current struggles. The sense of hurt so dominates their worlds that the brief relief self-injury offers them is their only respite—and they cannot imagine things will ever be different. For kids experiencing this level of pain, our responsibility is to model and communicate true hope.

Relational Response: Be a Protector and Advocate

Let's be honest: We're a long way from being able to ensure our kids have the safest possible environments in which to grow up. There's a lot of victimization of children and adolescents in our communities that must be surfaced. It goes on in playgrounds, schools, and all too often in the home. Of course, we have a legal and moral obligation to intervene in cases of abuse—and we must be vigilant in ensuring that the regulations and laws that surround this issue are carefully followed.

But there are other ways we can be involved. Simply by teaching young people to be kind to one another, we address a significant source of pain for kids who feel they don't fit. If you're in a position to influence individual kids or groups of teenagers, make it your mission to eliminate bullying, racial intolerance, backstabbing, gossip, and cliques. Look for ways to equip and empower parents in your community to relate to their own children in healthy ways. A few years ago I wrote down all the ideas I've used to help parents in a book called *Youth Worker's Guide to Parent Ministry (Zondervan, 2003)*. You might find some practical suggestions there that you can use in this important part of the work you do.

Relational Response: Challenge the Assumptions

We have tremendous opportunities for ministry among kids during their teenage years, when they are in the process of interpreting the painful experiences in their lives. Many kids are trying to come to terms with circumstances and events that seem to make no sense. Without loving mentors to help them think through what's going on around them, they will inevitably develop distorted and inaccurate interpretations—and we've seen how these distorted assumptions can serve as a driving force behind self-injuring behavior.

Our job is to intervene, to challenge the assumptions kids make about who they are in light of what's happening to them. Each of the destructive, paralyzing "I am" statements they want to embrace can be challenged.

When kids say, "I am worthless and unlovable,"

we must help them know they are precious and beloved.

When kids say, "I'm a pain and a burden,"

we must help them know they are gifted and needed.

When kids say, "I'm a stupid idiot,"

we must help them know they are wise and insightful.

When kids say, "I'm a misfit and a reject,"

we must help them know they belong and are wanted.

But here's the rub. It will not be through words alone that such deeply held assumptions can be challenged. If we want kids to understand themselves as precious and beloved and gifted and needed and wise and insightful and belonging and wanted, we must learn to communicate those truths relationally.

We must treat kids in ways that show them they are valued. We must offer them responsibilities and opportunities that show our belief in their gifts. We must listen carefully to their words so they'll know we respect their wisdom. We must welcome them warmly and communicate the kind of acceptance that continually reminds them they belong.

Breaking the Cycle

Remember the cycle of victimization and agency we looked at in chapter 8? I described it as a tornado that continually spirals downward into feelings of greater and greater chaos and relational isolation. Let me take you back to that illustration for just a moment. You'll remember that cycle doesn't leave a lot of room for hope:

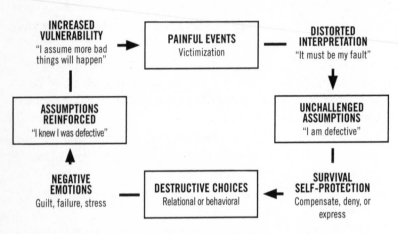

My dear friend Cal MacFarlane, professor of spiritual formation at Briercrest Seminary, describes another cycle that moves away from the downward spiral of victimization and agency we see all too often. He suggests that, in contrast to the downward spiral that leads to greater relational isolation, spiritual claustrophobia, and emotional chaos, there is a more hopeful cycle that can begin as kids learn to embrace the truth of who they are in Christ. When we can help kids see themselves as God sees them, we equip them with a new way to understand the pain they experience. And this opens their worlds to new possibilities, new friendships, new challenges, and a fresh new experience of the abundant life that Christ promises.

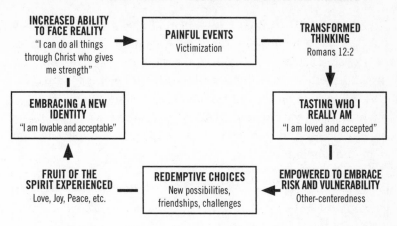

Of course, this doesn't change the fact that painful events still occur. The difference is that these events are now processed by a renewed mind, a mind transformed by the reality of God's love and acceptance. Instead of experiencing their pain as proof they are defective and unloved, their transformed thinking keeps these kids rooted in who they really are—beloved children of God.

In this new environment of love and acceptance, even deeply wounded young people can begin to choose to live and love more boldly. Instead of secrecy and self-protection their choices become redemptive. New and healthier relationships are formed. Possibilities that would have never been considered in the downward spiral can be enjoyed. And in the process, we begin to see more and more evidence of the Spirit of God at work in their lives. Instead of the familiar feelings of guilt and failure, we see glimpses of joy, peace, patience, and love emerging.

Gradually, a new identity is embraced. Over time, "I am loved and accepted" becomes "I am loveable and acceptable." In that radical new understanding, kids are empowered to face the reality of ongoing pain, disappointment, and hardship in a new way. With the Apostle Paul, they are able to declare, "I can do all things through Christ who gives me strength" (Philippians 4:13).

As we point kids to the truth of who they are in Christ, God can use us to break through Satan's cycle of lies and begin a new cycle of hope and healing. As we help kids discover they are accepted, loved, valued, and gifted, God works to free them from a life of bondage to their painful past and release them to a whole new way of living. This is the promise of the gospel for each of us—the truth of who we are in Christ that leads to freedom and wholeness.

> *"It is for freedom that Christ has set us free. Stand firm, then, and do not let yourselves be burdened again by a yoke of slavery." Galatians 5:1*

EPILOGUE

Remember Kelly? You met her in the first few pages of this book. Last night my wife and I bumped into her while we were out running some errands. Kelly immediately told us how hungry she was, so we invited her to grab a burger together with us.

It had been a tough day for Kelly. One of her close friends had committed suicide the night before, and she had a lot of emotions to process. She had tried to call her dad, but he was drunk and high. She hoped the high would wear off soon so she'd only have to deal with his drunkenness. "I know how to handle him when he's drunk," she told us. Her housing arrangements had fallen through the week before, so she was crashing at a friend's house. Things haven't improved much for her at school—the bullying from classmates goes on and teachers keep saying things that hurt her.

Yet even though Kelly's circumstances seem as messed up as ever, I left that McDonald's last night with some hope. It's been two and a half months since she last cut. That's the longest she's gone in years. "Put *that* in your book!" she said with a big freckled grin. "And by the way," she said. "I've been talking about God a lot with Michael, one of my friends from school. He's got a bunch of questions I can't answer. I need to get the three of us together soon so you can help him figure out all this stuff. I don't know where I'd be without God."

Kelly's heart for Jesus is so authentic it makes me smile. She got a job a month ago, is cutting back on cigarettes and is getting really serious about her photography hobby. The bizarre mixture of ups and downs in this kid's life leaves me shaking my head in disbelief most days. Could any roller coaster be wilder?

I wish I could know the end of Kelly's story. Right now it feels some days like she's hanging on by a thread, but my job isn't to speculate about the future. My job is to offer my presence in the midst of the chaos that is her young life.

When I work with kids like Kelly, I'm regularly reminded that I can't heal anyone. My role is that of an apprentice to the "Wonderful Counselor, Mighty God, Everlasting Father, Prince of Peace" (Isaiah 9:6). And every day I see him doing what only he can do—in my life and in the lives of the kids he brings into my office. There's no place I'd rather be.

BENEDICTION

Isaiah 53:2-5
(The Message)

There was nothing attractive about him,
nothing to cause us to take a second look.
He was looked down on and passed over,
a man who suffered, who knew pain firsthand.
One look at him and people turned away.
We looked down on him, thought he was scum.
But the fact is, it was our pains he carried—
our disfigurements, all the things wrong with us.
We thought he brought it on himself,
that God was punishing him for his own failures.
But it was our sins that did that to him,
that ripped and tore and crushed him—our sins!

He took the punishment, and that made us whole.
Through his bruises we get healed.

THE BILL OF RIGHTS FOR THOSE WHO SELF-HARM

"The Bill of Rights for Those Who Self-Harm" was created by Deb Martinson, an advocate for those who self-harm and chairperson of the American Self-Harm Information Clearinghouse. It addresses an often-overlooked issue in the way communities relate to people who self-injure. Its goal is to guarantee that people are treated with dignity and respect regardless of their specific issues. The tone is proactive, affirming, and respectful. I've included it because I believe the church has a great deal to learn about how we should treat people who don't fit neatly into our categories. It is reprinted with permission.

THE BILL OF RIGHTS FOR THOSE WHO SELF-HARM
Deb Martinson, ©1998-2001

1. The right to caring, humane medical treatment.
Self-injurers should receive the same level and quality of care that a person presenting with an identical but accidental injury would receive. Procedures should be done as gently as they would be for others. If stitches are required, local anesthesia should be used. Treatment of accidental injury and self-inflicted injury should be identical.

2. The right to participate fully in decisions about emergency psychiatric treatment (so long as no one's life is in immediate danger).

When a person presents at the emergency room with a self-inflicted injury, his or her opinion about the need for a psychological assessment should be considered. If the person is not in obvious distress and is not suicidal, he or she should not be subjected to an arduous psych evaluation. Doctors should be trained to assess suicidality/homicidality and should realize that although referral for outpatient follow-up may be advisable, hospitalization for self-injurious behavior alone is rarely warranted.

3. The right to body privacy.

Visual examinations to determine the extent and frequency of self-inflicted injury should be performed only when absolutely necessary and done in a way that maintains the patient's dignity. Many who SI have been abused; the humiliation of a strip-search is likely to increase the amount and intensity of future self-injury while making the person subject to the searches look for better ways to hide the marks.

4. The right to have the feelings behind the SI validated.

Self-injury doesn't occur in a vacuum. The person who self-injures usually does so in response to distressing feelings, and those feelings should be recognized and validated. Although the care provider might not understand why a particular situation is extremely upsetting, she or he can at least understand that it is distressing and respect the self-injurer's right to be upset about it.

5. The right to disclose to whom they choose only what they choose.

No care provider should disclose to others that injuries are self-inflicted without obtaining the permission of the person involved. Exceptions can be made in the case of team-based hospital treatment or other medical care providers when the information that the injuries were self-inflicted is essential knowledge for proper medical care. Patients should be notified when others are told about their SI and, as always, gossiping about any patient is unprofessional.

6. The right to choose what coping mechanisms they will use.

No person should be forced to choose between self-injury and treatment. Outpatient therapists should never demand that clients sign a no-harm contract; instead, client and provider should develop a plan for dealing with self-injurious impulses and acts during the treatment. No client should feel they must lie about SI or be kicked out of outpatient therapy. Exceptions to this may be made in hospital or ER treatment, when a contract may be required by hospital legal policies.

7. The right to have care providers who do not allow their feelings about SI to distort the therapy.

Those who work with clients who self-injure should keep their own fear, revulsion, anger, and anxiety out of the therapeutic setting. This is crucial for basic medical care of self-inflicted wounds but holds for therapists as well. A person who is struggling with self-injury has enough baggage without taking on the prejudices and biases of their care providers.

8. The right to have the role SI has played as a coping mechanism validated.

No one should be shamed, admonished, or chastised for having self-injured. Self-injury works as a coping mechanism, sometimes for people who have no other way to cope. They may use SI as a last-ditch effort to avoid suicide. The self-injurer should be taught to honor the positive things that self-injury has done for him/her as well as to recognize that the negatives of SI far outweigh those positives and that it is possible to learn methods of coping that aren't as destructive and life-interfering.

9. The right not to be automatically considered a dangerous person simply because of self-inflicted injury.

No one should be put in restraints or locked in a treatment room in an emergency room solely because his or her injuries are self-inflicted. No one should ever be involuntarily committed simply because of SI; physicians should make the decision to commit based on the presence of psychosis, suicidality, or homicidality.

10. The right to have self-injury regarded as an attempt to communicate, not manipulate.

Most people who hurt themselves are trying to express things they can say in no other way. Although sometimes these attempts to communicate seem manipulative, treating them as manipulation only makes the situation worse. Providers should respect the communicative function of SI and assume it is not manipulative behavior until there is clear evidence to the contrary.

The organizations and Web sites below include a diverse range of points of view. While I believe all these have value, they should be viewed with discernment. I'd urge helpers to be especially cautious about sending self-injuring kids to Web sites you haven't checked out first or recommending organizations with which you are unfamiliar.

ORGANIZATIONS

To Write Love on Her Arms (www.twloha.com/index.php)

To Write Love on Her Arms is a movement to raise awareness around issues of depression and self-injury. It offers hope and challenges people to truly believe they can make a difference in the lives of those who seem to have lost all hope.

S.A.F.E. Alternatives® (www.selfinjury.com/index.html)

S.A.F.E. Alternatives® (Self-Abuse Finally Ends) is a nationally recognized treatment approach, professional network, and educational resource base committed to helping self-injurers and those who love them achieve an end to self-injurious behavior.

S.A.F.E. in Canada (not affiliated with S.A.F.E. Alternatives in the U.S.) (www.safeincanada.ca)

S.A.F.E. in Canada says its mission is "to reduce the burden of suffering caused by self-injury." It does so by working directly with those who self-injure, and by helping their families, their friends, and the professionals who care for them.

Equilibrium (www.selfharmony.com.uk)

Based in the United Kingdom, Equilibrium is an award-winning user-led self-injury awareness group that seeks to help educate and support people who self-harm, as well as their family and friends.

LifeSIGNS (www.lifesigns.org.uk)

LifeSIGNS (Self-Injury Guidance & Network Support) is an online, volunteer-led organization, founded in 2002. It seeks to raise awareness about self-injury and provide information and support to people of all ages affected by self-injury.

WEB SITES

www.psyke.org

This Web site includes information about self-injury, and suggestions on books and resources regarding coping and recovery, as well as poetry, personal stories, and photos from individuals who self-injure. Be sure to take a close look at this site before recommending it to kids. The poetry and photos might push kids who are vulnerable to self-injurious behavior in negative directions if there is no one to walk through it with them.

www.cutthemovie.com

Here's the Web site for a documentary film called *CUT: Teens and Self-Injury*, which has been described as "an intimate and profoundly moving look at a largely unspoken issue affecting thousands of young people." The site includes background about the film as well as information about ordering it.

www.helpguide.org/mental/self_injury.htm

This site offers an overview of the types, causes, and treatment of self-injury. It includes information on the factors that can lead to self-injury, suggestions for helping a loved one who self-injures, and a list of resources.

www.selfharm.org.uk/default.aspa

Another informational site that seeks to serve as "a key information resource for young people who self-harm, their friends and families, and professionals working with them."

www.siari.co.uk

"SIARI provides one of the most comprehensive sources of information and resources currently available on self-injury/self-harm and related issues. The site will be of value to anyone wishing to gain insight into the complex and much-misunderstood phenomenon of self-injury, and the issues that surround it."

www.mayoclinic.com/health/self-injury/DS00775

This page is part of the Web site of the well-known Mayo Clinic. It introduces self-injury, discusses signs, symptoms, and diagnosis, and provides helpful information on how to respond. It comes primarily from a medical perspective.

www.self-injury.net

This site was created by a 27-year-old woman who is a self-injurer. It includes a section of frequently asked questions about self-injury, with responses from self-injurers. It also includes resources and advice for families and friends of self-injurers.

www.youthnoise.com/page.php?page_id=1419

Here's a "for youth, by youth" site that includes the "Top 10 Myths about Self-Injury" and links and information on where to find further help.

www.palace.net/~llama/psych/injury.html

This Web site called "Secret Shame (Self-Injury Information and Support)" provides a wide variety of information on self-injury including basic facts, causes, information for families/friends, quotes, and references, as well as other resources.

www.selfmutilatorsanonymous.org

Self-Mutilators Anonymous is "a fellowship of men and women who share their experience, strength, and hope with each other, so that they may solve their common problem and help others recover from physical self-mutilation." The site includes dates, times, addresses, and contact information for group meetings around the world (mostly in the United States and Canada).

FOR FURTHER READING: ADDITIONAL BOOKS ON SELF-INJURY

A number of excellent resources on the topic of self-injury have been developed over the last decade or so. This brief bibliography will introduce you to the books I've found to be most helpful. In my opinion the best two books about self-injury are *A Bright Red Scream* by Merilee Strong and *Inside a Cutter's Mind* by Jerusha Clark and Dr. Earl Henslin.

Alderman, Tracy, Ph.D. *The Scarred Soul: Understanding and Ending Self-Inflicted Violence.* Oakland: New Harbinger Publications, 1997.

This book was written to those who self-harm, as well as their therapists, families, and friends, and is meant to help people end their destructive patterns. Alderman wants people to be able to step away from secrecy and toward reawakening their emotions and overall healing. She starts by explaining what self-inflicted violence is, why people do it, and the nature of it. She also examines cycles and psychological factors. The book discusses how to end self-harm and gives a whole section on the role others can play in a self-injurer's process of healing.

Carlson, Melody. *Blade Silver.* Colorado Springs: TH1NK, 2005.

Carlson approaches the topic of self-injury through a novel—a new genre for books on the subject. Written as a memoir with an older teen-age or young adult audience in mind, this book offers a fresh approach and is a great tool for starting discussions on the topic of self-injury. Readers will relate to the honesty with which the story is written. It's believable and leads to a resolution that will communicate hope to readers who find themselves struggling with these issues.

Clark, Jerusha. *Inside a Cutter's Mind.* **With Dr. Earl Henslin.** Colorado Springs: TH1NK, 2007.

One of the first substantial books on self-injury written from a Christian perspective, this book is a great resource. Clark's approach is thoughtfully biblical and highly practical, while Henslin adds a technical credibility that makes this an important book for counselors, parents, and youth workers to have on their shelves. The research is thorough and the case studies throughout the book illustrate the points extremely well. This book truly points to the hope that can be found in the healing relationship with Christ.

Conterio, Karen, and Wendy Lader, Ph.D. *Bodily Harm: The Breakthrough Healing Program for Self-Injurers.* New York: Hyperion, 1998.

This book is written by the directors of the S.A.F.E. (Self-Abuse Finally Ends) Alternatives® program, which is perhaps the most comprehensive and widely available strategy for addressing self-harm. The first half of the book contains general information on self-injury and looks at the con-nections to eating disorders, child abuse, and early trauma. It also spe-cifically examines the biological implications, adolescent self-harm, body image, and the male self-injurer. Family characteristics and medical con-siderations are also addressed. The second half of the book describes the approach of the S.A.F.E. Alternatives® program and why it works.

Favazza, Armando R., M.D. *Bodies under Siege: Self-Mutilation and Body Modification in Culture and Psychiatry,* **2nd ed.** London: The Johns Hopkins University Press, 1996.

Here's one of the early technical texts that addressed the issue of self-injury. Favazza was one of the first to acknowledge self-harm for what it actually is. Like several other books on this list, Favazza's book uses the term *self-mutilation* (a term now considered offensive by most self-injurers), yet it's filled with helpful information. He begins by looking at mutilative beliefs, religion, eating, and ethology. He then moves to the mutilation of body parts (cultural and clinical cases). He concludes with discernment and therapy, which includes understanding self-mutilation, biological and psychosocial findings, and treatment. This is a useful text for those interested in the history of research in this field and are looking for technical information.

Kettlewell, Caroline. *Skin Game: A Memoir.* New York: St. Martin's Press, 1999.
This is one of the first autobiographical accounts of self-harm. Kettlewell is a brilliant writer who expresses her thoughts in vivid word pictures and carefully crafted phrases. It's worth reading the book just to be exposed to her fine writing style. The book chronicles approximately 20 years of her story, in which she reveals her journey of self-discovery and, ultimately, recovery. The book is full of insightful and powerful quotes that allow the reader a glimpse into the mind of a cutter.

Leatham, Victoria. *Bloodletting: A Memoir of Secrets, Self-Harm and Survival.* Oakland: New Harbinger Publications, 2006.
Another vivid autobiographical memoir, darkly humorous and often chilling in its detail and candor. Leatham allows us into her mind and reveals her most intimate thoughts as she struggles with cutting and a range of other psychological problems. The topic is depressing but the writing is delightful and the insights you'll gain from hearing Leatham's reflections on a life of dysfunction will help you better understand those who self-harm.

Levenkron, Steven. *Cutting: Understanding and Overcoming Self-Mutilation.* New York: W. W. Norton and Company, 1998.
Steven Levenkron wrote this book for those who self-harm and their parents, friends, and therapists. His goal is to explain the "why" behind the disorder and show people how self-injurers can be helped. Levenkron has been working in the field since 1976, so he is extremely qualified. In the first part of his book he explains the phenomenon

of self-harm and explains the benefits and value that people find in cutting. The second section of his book revolves around the road to recovery. This was one of the first easily readable books written on the subject.

Ng, Gina. *Everything You Need to Know about Self-Mutilation: A Helping Book for Teens Who Hurt Themselves.* New York: The Rosen Publishing Group, 1998.

This short booklet (only about 60 pages) was written for teens on the subject of self-harm. There are pictures and the text is easy to read, explaining the dynamics of self-injury in a way most teenagers will understand. It shows the consequences of cutting and profiles those who do it. The book also looks at getting help and where to go. It includes a glossary at the back, defining key terms associated with self-injury.

Strong, Marilee. *A Bright Red Scream: Self-Mutilation and the Language of Pain.* New York: Viking, 1998.

This is one of the most readily available and accessible books on the subject of self-injury. It's an ideal first book to read because it's full of case illustrations that highlight the dynamics and challenges of dealing with self-injury. The book is well documented and well written. Strong helps us understand not only self-injury, but also its relationship to childhood trauma, sexual abuse, and eating disorders.

Turner, V. J. *Secret Scars: Uncovering and Understanding the Addiction of Self-Injury.* Center City, MN: Hazelden, 2002.

This book examines self-harm as an addiction. It has useful information on numerous facets of cutting including background factors, historical indicators, the reasons for the recent increase, treatment options, spirituality, writing tools, and healing. The book is written for cutters, people who know cutters and want to help, counselors, psychologists, doctors, and teachers. A very helpful resource for people who want technical information in a readable form.

CUT
BY
DAVE TIPPETT

This reader's theater by Dave Tippett is a practical tool that can be used to start a conversation about self-injury in a way that is redemptive and hopeful. The drama reinforces a number of the concepts in this book. If you are interested in seeing more of Dave's work, which deals with the tough issues kids face on a daily basis, you can contact him at Djtipp@aol.com.

Running Time: 5-6 minutes

Theme: The scars we inflict.

Scripture: Isaiah 53:5

Synopsis: Reader's theater. A teenager tells her story of self-injuring and the Savior's healing scars.

Cast: Four READERS. All teen girls.

Setting: Empty stage. Four teen girls standing, one at each corner of the stage.

Props: None

R1: It was really weird at first.

R2: It was like this—

R3: —impulsive thing.

R4: I didn't plan it.

R1: It was a really bad time—

R2: —in my life.

R3: And I didn't know what to do or—

R4: —who to talk to.

R1: So, I just—

UNISON: —did it.

R4: It got my mind off my stuff.

R1: It took me to a—

R2: —better place.

R3: —better place.

R4: —better place.
(pause)

R1: I bled a lot. The first time.

R2: A lot.

R3: I went too deep.

R4: Rookie mistake.

R1: I was a lot more careful—

R2: —the next time—

R3: —and the time after that.

R4: —and that—

UNISON: —and on.
(pause)

R1: I wasn't trying to kill myself—

R2: —or anything. But—

R3: —every time I felt awful about something—

R4: —I'd do it again.

R1: And again. Soon—

R2: —it became—

UNISON: —habit.
(pause)

R3: The cut.

R4: Cutting.

R1: Cutting my body.

R2: Didn't hurt. It was more of a—

UNISON: —relief.

R1: I…I—

R2: Sometimes imagined they were—

R3: —the same cuts Jesus had on him. 'Cept—

R4: Mine felt deeper.

UNISON: Or so I thought.
(pause)

R1: Weird, huh?
(pause)

R1: After a while, I began to—

R2: —like—

R3: —the way the cuts looked. On me.

R4: And started hating when they—

R1: —healed up.

R2: I'd find myself—

R3: —freshening them up.

R4: They were like my own way of—

UNISON: —controlling things—

R1: —in an uncontrollable world.
(pause)

R1: One day, I cut too deep.

R2: It wasn't pretty.

R3: I was OK, but it showed me—

R4: —this had to stop. And, because—

R1: —it wasn't working anymore. It wasn't healing—

R2: —anything.

R3: They were too deep, the scars.

R4: Too deep. (pause) Jesus had—

R1: —wounds too. But, I found out, later—

R2: —his went much deeper. And could—

R3: —heal—

UNISON: —all scars.
(pause)

R3: I finally—

R4: —told someone.

R1: Someone—

R2: —who knew about the cuts of Christ—

R3: —and the only blood that mattered.

R4: She got me help. To see—

R1: —that the stuff in my life—

R2: —couldn't be cured with cutting.

R3: But letting the scars truly—

R4: —heal.

R1: For good.
(pause)

R2: It took a long time.
(pause)

R1: Now, I don't cut—

R2: —myself—

R3: —anymore.
(pause)

R4: Sometimes, I get—

R1: —tempted. But.

R1: My scars have healed over.

R2: His scars have sealed the wounds.

R3: Crucified with Him, now—

R4: —in many ways—

R1: —and hoping, and—

R2: —praying—

R3: —praying—

R4: —praying—

UNISON: —he'll keep control.